THE LANGUAGE OF
POST-MODERN ARCHITECTURE

THE LANGUAGE OF
POST-MODERN ARCHITECTURE

CHARLES A. JENCKS

ACADEMY EDITIONS · LONDON

An *Architectural Design* Monograph

To Maggie Keswick

Frontispiece
KISHO KUROKAWA, *Nakagin Capsule Building,* Tokyo, 1972. (Tomio Ohashi).

First published in Great Britain in 1977 by
Academy Editions, 7 Holland Street, London W8

Copyright © 1977 Charles Jencks. *All rights reserved*

SBN Cloth: 85670 320 6   SBN Paper: 85670 325 7

Printed in Great Britain by
Balding & Mansell Ltd., Wisbech, England

CONTENTS

INTRODUCTION . . . 7

PART ONE **The Death of Modern Architecture** . . . 9

Crisis in architecture . . . 10
Univalent form . . . 15
Univalent formalists and inadvertent symbolists . . . 19
Univalent content . . . 25

PART TWO **The Modes of Architectural Communication** . . . 39

Metaphor . . . 40
Words . . . 60
Syntax . . . 72
Semantics . . . 73

PART THREE **Post-Modern Architecture** . . . 87

Recent departures . . . 87
Multivalent architecture . . . 96

NOTES . . . 102

INDEX . . . 103

1 RICARDO BOFILL and TALLER, *Walden Seven,* Barcelona, 1975.

INTRODUCTION

The phrase 'post-modern' is not the most happy expression one can use concerning recent architecture. It is evasive, fashionable and worst of all negative – like defining women as 'non-men'. It doesn't say immediately, like a good slogan, what banner to follow, or like 'The New Brutalism' what particular 'ism' should be emulated. All it admits is the minimum information that certain architects and buildings have moved beyond or counter to modern architecture. And yet it is precisely this vagueness and implied pluralism which the title of this book is meant to convey. The present situation tolerates opposite approaches, and I hope that architecture doesn't prematurely crystallise around a single style and doctrinaire approach, as it has so many times in this century. If there is a single direction I prefer, the reader will discover that it is pluralistic: the idea that an architect must master several styles and codes of communication and vary these to suit the particular culture for which he is designing. I have called this 'adhocism' in the past, and I use the term 'radical eclecticism' here to give this approach a name, but there are other portmanteau terms which would work: 'Traditionalesque', 'Neo-Art Nouveau', 'Anthropologism'. There is obviously good reason for avoiding such unwieldy labels at this stage.

This book commences with what is now becoming a standard attack on the modern movement. If I have anything to add to the rising vituperation, it is the notion that a failure of recent architecture has been one of communication. After questioning the theory of communication that supported modern architecture, I switch from polemic and caricature to a discussion of the way an architect can signify those meanings he intended in a building.

But I should emphasise what this discussion leaves out: except for a few instances, it excludes the interiors of buildings, with all those signs of comfort and habitation and daily life which are so important in giving meaning to architecture. My concentration on the exterior and visual meanings is meant to stand for the missing area, and to be applied to it by analogy. The lessons of visual communication can be extended to other areas, and I have concentrated on them because they are the most potent in architecture (we don't ordinarily judge a building by its smell). Also, visual meanings are more easy to represent in a book than tactile, acoustic and spatial qualities, which are best conveyed in film. I have not discussed architecture in China, or indeed much outside of the Anglo-European context (except for Japan). The reason is, inevitably, that I am most acquainted with English and American developments. Lastly, my classification of subcultures, or 'semiotic groups', is very general and not meant to be taken as the last word in sociological analysis (as I'm sure it won't be).

Bringing up the subject of semiotics immediately broaches the question of linguistics: how much can architecture be a language? I will not answer this question in depth, but leave it to another book, an anthology *Signs, Symbols and Architecture* which will appear sometime later. The anthology is more technical and scholarly, looking at architectural language from the standpoint of semiotics – the theory of signs, or the general theory of how everything can communicate, from women's clothing to wrestling matches. This book, by contrast, tries to apply the theories of semiotics in a loose way to existing architecture. What may have been lost in precision, is hopefully gained in immediacy, but the reader should be warned that terms are not being used in a technical sense and that there is a whole body of erudite literature devoted to the questions raised here.

A personal remark to clear up possible ambiguities. Since I have written several books which partly defended modern architecture, some critics will find this one irreconcilable with the previous ones. No doubt my position has been modified under the influences of critics such as Jane Jacobs, by the growing disenchantment with modern architecture in general, and also in being confronted with the depressing evidence first-hand; but my attitude hasn't changed altogether. I wouldn't reject modern architecture *in toto*, as certain critics would, but rather hope to see it confined to a much smaller area, a local and perhaps elite taste culture. Modern architecture took every culture as its province, it claimed to be universal; and under the pressure of fashion, technology and specious argument, these claims have led to its indiscriminate practice around the world. It's rather as if world leaders took the inflated claims of Esperanto seriously and had this ahistorical, logical language spoken in every major city. We wouldn't be conversing with much pleasure, elegance or wit. Yet there are limited areas where modern architecture can be appropriate and effective: certainly in large engineering structures, probably many impersonal building types, such as offices; and where the individual may choose it – in the *private* house. Certainly not mass housing, nor large-scale urban redevelopment. In short, its claims to universality should be exposed as ideological, and modern architecture should be put quickly in its semantic place – where it belongs with respect to other styles and approaches.

Conrad Jameson's wholesale attack on modern architecture and his argument in favour of a return to pattern books clarified the issue of using traditional models as a starting point for design. Many old modern architects are moving backwards at a snail's pace, and he showed me how much more speedy and efficient their reverse gear should be. For this and for editorial advice, I thank him, even if I can't finally agree with his total demolition job.

Maggie Keswick also changed my opinions in many instances, particularly after we'd both visited a modern building and haggled over our different impressions. Because her ideas have so clearly infected mine, I would like to dedicate to her all those parts of the book with which she would agree and leave the rest as my sole responsibility.

Also my thanks go to Haig Beck and Andreas Papadakis who helped initiate, edit and publish the text, and the editors of *The Sunday Times*, the *Architectural Association Quarterly* and *Architectural Design,* in which several parts have appeared in a different form.

Charles Jencks, London
September, 1976

2 MORRIS LAPIDUS, *Eden Roc Hotel,* Miami, 1954. Lapidus started the Ersatz styling of large hotels with his confections during the fifties in Florida. He mixes all the popular periods of interior design – Louis XIV, Robert Adam, Moderne Streamlined – in a distinctive but unclassifiable style. This one is 'it-could-be-Baroque'. Lapidus came to this commercial formula through shop designs, and now it has been applied with success throughout the world – as the following London hotels show. (Morris Lapidus Associates, Architects).

PART ONE
The Death of Modern Architecture

Happily, we can date the death of modern architecture to a precise moment in time. Unlike the legal death of a person, which is becoming a complex affair of brain waves versus heartbeats, modern architecture went out with a bang. That many people didn't notice, and no one was seen to mourn, does not make the sudden extinction any less of a fact, and that many designers are still trying to administer the kiss of life does not mean that it has been miraculously resurrected. No, it expired finally and completely in 1972, after having been flogged to death remorselessly for ten years by critics such as Jane Jacobs; and the fact that many so-called modern architects still go around practising a trade as if it were alive can be taken as one of the great curiosities of our age (like the British Monarchy giving life-prolonging drugs to 'The Royal Company of Archers' or 'The Extra Women of the Bedchamber').

Modern Architecture died in St Louis, Missouri on July 15, 1972 at 3.32 p.m. (or thereabouts) when the infamous Pruitt-Igoe scheme, or rather several of its slab
3 blocks, were given the final *coup de grâce* by dynamite. Previously it had been vandalised, mutilated and defaced by its black inhabitants, and although millions of dollars were pumped back, trying to keep it alive (fixing the broken elevators, repairing smashed windows, repainting), it was finally put out of its misery. Boom, boom, boom.

Without doubt, the ruins should be kept, the remains should have a preservation order slapped on them, so that
4 we keep a live memory of this failure in planning and architecture. Like the folly or artificial ruin – constructed on the estate of an eighteenth-century English eccentric to provide him with instructive reminders of former vanities and glories – we should learn to value and protect our former disasters. As Oscar Wilde said, 'experience is the name we give to our mistakes', and there is a certain health in leaving them judiciously scattered around the landscape as continual lessons.

Pruitt-Igoe was constructed according to the most progressive ideals of CIAM (the Congress of International Modern Architects) and it won an award from the American Institute of Architects when it was designed in 1951. It consisted of elegant slab blocks fourteen storeys high with rational 'streets in the air' (which were safe from cars, but as it turned out, not safe from crime); 'sun, space and greenery', which Le Corbusier called the 'three essential joys of urbanism' (instead of conventional streets, gardens and semi-private space, which he banished). It had a separation of pedestrian and vehicular traffic, the provision of play space, and local amenities such as laundries, crèches and gossip centres – all rational substitutes for traditional patterns. Moreover, its Purist style, its clean, salubrious hospital metaphor, was meant to instil, by good example, corresponding virtues in the inhabitants. Good form was to lead to good content, or at least good conduct; the intelligent planning of abstract space was to promote healthy behaviour.

3 MINORU YAMASAKI, *Pruitt-Igoe Housing*, St Louis, 1952–55. Several slab blocks of this scheme were blown up in 1972 after they were continuously vandalised. The crime rate was higher than other developments, and Oscar Newman attributed this, in his book *Defensible Space*, to the long corridors, anonymity, and lack of controlled semi-private space. Another factor: it was designed in a purist language at variance with the architectural codes of the inhabitants.

4 PRUITT-IGOE AS RUIN. Like the Berlin Wall and the collapse of the high-rise block, Ronan Point, in England, 1968, this ruin has become a great architectural symbol. It should be preserved as a warning. Actually, after continued hostilities and disagreements, some blacks have managed to form a community in parts of the remaining habitable blocks – another symbol, in its way, that events and ideology, as well as architecture, determine the success of the environment.

5 RICHARD SEIFERT, *Penta Hotel,* London, 1972. The English government subsidised these kinds of hotels in the late sixties to cope with the tourist boom. Twenty or so, with about 500 bedrooms, sprang up on the main route in from the airport. On the outside they are uptight International Style, on the inside Lapidus Ersatz. (R. Seifert & Partners).

6 PENTA HOTEL, interior themed in the Vassarely-Airport-Lounge style. The irony that the same interiors could be found where the tourist left home has not escaped many critics. Nonetheless this tradition continues to thrive.

Alas, such simplistic ideas, taken over from philosophic doctrines of Rationalism, Behaviourism and Pragmatism, proved as irrational as the philosophies themselves. Modern Architecture, as the son of the Enlightenment, was an heir to its congenital naivities, naivities too great and awe-inspiring to warrant refutation in a book on mere building. I will concentrate here, in this first part, on the demise of a very small branch of a big bad tree; but to be fair it should be pointed out that modern architecture is the offshoot of modern painting, the modern movements in all the arts. Like rational schooling, rational health and rational design of women's bloomers, it has the faults of an age trying to reinvent itself totally on rational grounds. These shortcomings are now well known, thanks to the writings of Ivan Illich, Jacques Ellul, E. F. Schumacher, Michael Oakshott and Hannah Arendt, and the overall misconceptions of Rationalism will not be dwelt upon. They are assumed for my purposes. Rather than a deep extended attack on modern architecture, showing how its ills relate very closely to the prevailing philosophies of the modern age, I will attempt a caricature, a polemic. The virtue of this genre (as well as its vice) is its license to cut through the large generalities with a certain abandon and enjoyment, overlooking all the exceptions and subtleties of the argument. Caricature is of course not the whole truth. Daumier's drawings didn't really show what nineteenth-century poverty was about, but rather gave a highly selective view of *some* truths. Let us then romp through the desolation of modern architecture, and the destruction of our cities, like some Martian tourist out on an earthbound excursion, visiting the archaeological sites with a superior disinterest, bemused by the sad but instructive mistakes of a former architectural civilisation. After all, since it is fairly dead, we might as well enjoy picking over the corpse.

Crisis in architecture

In 1974 Malcolm MacEwen wrote a book of the above title which summarised the English view of what was wrong with the Modern Movement (capitalised, like all world religions), and what we should do about it. His summary was masterful, but his prescriptions were wildly off the mark: the remedy was to overhaul a tiny institutional body, the Royal Institute of British Architects, by changing a style here and a heart there – as if these sorts of things would make the *multiple causes* of the crisis go away. Well, let me make use of his effective analysis, not his solution, taking as a typical grotesque of modern architecture one building type: modern hotels.

The new Penta Hotel in London has 914 bedrooms, 5
which is almost nine times the average large hotel of
fifty years ago, and it is 'themed' (a word of decorators)
in the International Style and a mode which could be
called Vassarely-Airport-Lounge-Moderne. There are 6
about twenty of these leviathans near each other, on the
way to the London Airport (it is known in the trade as
'Hotellandia'), and they create a disruption in scale and
city life which amounts to the occupation of an invading
army – a role tourists tend to fulfil.

These newly formed battalions with their noble-phoney
names include The Churchill (500 bedrooms, named after 7
Sir Winston and themed in the Pompeian-Palladian Style
by way of Robert Adam); the Imperial Hotel (720 bedrooms, International outside, fibreglass Julius Caesar
inside); and the Park Tower (300 bedrooms, themed in 8
Corn-on-the-Cob and various sunburst motifs inside).

7 The CHURCHILL HOTEL, London, 1971. A typical combination of revival style with modern services. The brochure reads: 'Your car glides to a stop under the cover of the *porte cochère*. The door is opened. Your fleeting glance sees faces . . . uniforms . . . a hand touching a hat brim in half salute . . . good evening, sir . . . this way, please . . . and you enter the lobby. Before you stretches a hall. Cool and distant and almost white. Crystal chandeliers bathe the marble floors and columns in soft white light. There are people but it is rather quiet. Composed feelings. And elegant. This is the Churchill.' If Robert Adam only had air-conditioners and down lighters he might have achieved something as cool and distant too.

8 RICHARD SEIFERT, *The Park Tower,* London, 1973. Compared to a gasometre, stacked television sets, and corn-on-the-cob, this modelled exterior was an attempt to get away from the flat facade. The interior is themed with the stock-in-trade sunburst motif. (R. Seifert & Partners).

A recurring aspect of these hotels, built between 1969 and 1973, is that they provide very modern services, such as air-conditioning, themed in old-world styles which vary from Rococco, Gothic, Second Empire, to a com-
9 bination of all three styles together. The formula of ancient style and modern plumbing has proved inexorably successful in our consumer society, and this Ersatz has been the major commercial challenge to classical modern architecture. But in one important way, in terms of architectural *production*, Ersatz and modern architecture contribute equally to alienation and what MacEwen calls 'the crisis'. I have tried to untangle the different causes of this situation, at least eleven in number, and show how they operate in the two modern modes of architectural
10 production (listed in the two right hand columns of the diagram).

For contrast, the first column on the left refers to the old system of *private* architectural production (operating largely before World War One) where an architect knew his client personally, probably shared his values and aesthetic code. An extreme example of this is Lord Burlington's Chiswick Villa, an unusual situation where the architect was the builder (or contractor), client and user all at once. Hence there was no disparity between his rather elite and esoteric code (a spare, intellectual version of the Palladian language) and his way of life. The same identity exists today, although on a more modest scale and as a relative rarity – the 'Handmade Houses' which are built outside urban centres in America, or the boat house community in Sausalito, in San Francisco Bay, where

9 AIR-CONDITIONING at the *Elizabetta Hotel* 1972. The incorporation of many modern services – electric candelabra, muzak, surveillance systems, telephone, alarm bell, elevators – within Ersatz styles produces incongruous juxtapositions. A surreal humour is sometimes sought, although underplayed. The ingenuity is undeniable, and some hotels, like the Elizabetta, have the courage of their own vulgarity.

10 'CRISIS IN ARCHITECTURE' a diagram of three systems of architectural production. The left column shows the implications of the old, private system of production, while the right columns show the two modern systems. Critics of modern architecture have emphasised several of these eleven causes of the crisis, but clearly the causes are multiple and work as a *system* tied into the economic sphere. The question is – how many variables must be changed for the system to change?

		SYSTEM 1 — PRIVATE private architect / client is user	SYSTEM 2 — PUBLIC public architect / client and users differ	SYSTEM 3 — DEVELOPER developer architect / client and users differ
1	ECONOMIC SPHERE	**Mini-Capitalist** (restricted money)	**Welfare-State Capitalist** (lacks money)	**Monopoly-Capitalist** (has money)
2	MOTIVATION	aesthetic ideological | inhabit use	solve problem | user's housing	make money | make money to use
3	RECENT IDEOLOGY	Too various to list	progress, efficiency, large scale, anti-history, Brutalism, etc.	Same as System 2 plus pragmatic
4	RELATION TO PLACE	local architect | client user in place	remote architects / users move to place	remote and changing draughtsmen | absent clients
5	CLIENT'S RELATION TO ARCHITECT	**Expert Friend** same partners small team	**Anonymous Doctor** changing designers large team	**Hired Servant** doesn't know designers or users
6	SIZE OF PROJECTS	**"small"**	**"some large"**	**"too big"**
7	SIZE/TYPE OF ARCHITECT'S OFFICE	small partnership	large centralised	large centralised
8	METHOD OF DESIGN	slow, responsive, innovative, expensive	impersonal, anonymous, conservative, low cost	quick, cheap, and proven formulae
9	ACCOUNTABILITY	to client-user	to local council and bureaucracy	to stockholders, developers and board
10	TYPES OF BUILDING	houses, museums, universities, etc.	housing and infrastructure	shopping centres, hotels, offices, factories, etc.
11	STYLE	**multiple**	**impersonal** safe, contemporary, vandal-proofed	**pragmatic** cliché and bombastic

each boat house is built by the inhabitant in a different,
11 personalised style. These self-built houses testify to the close correspondence there can be between meaning and form when architectural production is at a small scale and controlled by the inhabitant.

Other factors which influenced this type of production in the past include the *mini-capitalist economy* where money was restricted. The architect or speculative builder designed relatively *small* parts of the city at one go; he worked *slowly*, responding to well-established needs, and he was *accountable* to the client, who was invariably the user of the building as well. All these factors, and more that are shown in the diagram, combined to produce an architecture understood by the client and in a language shared by others.

The second and third columns refer to the way most architecture is produced today and show why it is out of scale with historic cities, and alienating to both architects and society. First, in the economic sphere, it's either produced for a public welfare agency which lacks the money necessary to carry out the socialist intentions of the architects, or it is funded by a capitalist agency whose monopoly creates gigantic investments and correspondingly gigantic buildings. For instance, the Penta Hotel is owned by the European Hotel Corporation, a consortium of five airlines and five international banks. These ten corporations together create a monolith which by financial definition must appeal to mass taste, at a middle-class
12 level. There is nothing inherently inferior about this taste culture; it's rather the economic imperatives determining the size and predictability of the result which have coerced the architecture into becoming so relentlessly pretentious and uptight.

Secondly, in this type of production, the architect's motivation is either to solve a problem, or in the case of the developer's architect, to make money. Why the latter motivation doesn't produce effective architecture as it did in the past remains a mystery, (unless it is connected with the compelling pressures of predictable taste). But it is quite clear why 'problems' don't produce architecture. They produce instead 'rational' solutions to oversimplified questions in a chaste style.

Yet the greatest cause of alienation is the *size* of today's projects: the hotels, garages, shopping centres and housing estates which are 'too big' – like the architectural offices which produce them. How big is too big? Obviously there is no easy answer to this, and we await the detailed study of different building types. But the equation can be formulated in general, and it might be called 'the Ivan Illich Law of Diminishing Architecture' (parallel to his discoveries of counter-productive growth in other fields). It could be stated as follows: 'for any building type there is an upper limit to the number of people who can be served before the quality of the environment falls'. The service of the large London hotels has fallen because of staff shortages and absenteeism, and the quality of tourism has declined because the tourists are treated as so many cattle to be shunted from one ambience to the
13 next in a smooth and continuous flow. Programmed,

11 SAUSALITO BAY BOAT HOUSES, 1960– . Like the Handmade Houses of California, these boat houses depend on the oldest form of architectural production – *self-build*. Each one is tailor-made by the inhabitant in a different style, and you find cheek-by-jowl, a Swiss chalet boat house and a converted caravan, or here, the Venturi style next to the A-frame Fuller style.

12 PENTA RESTAURANT interior with its royal, fibreglass cartouche *Dieu-et-mon-droit*. Actually Holiday Inns, the biggest multinational in hotels, prefabricates these fibreglass symbols and then sends them out to some of their 1,700 concessions. The multinationals have been instrumental in standardising world taste and creating a world 'consumption community'. The National Biscuit Company foresees the goal of two billion biscuit munchers eating their standard average cookie.

13 DISNEYLAND, opened in 1955 as a dream of Walt Disney, started the new form of ride-through parks where people are put on a continuously moving assembly line and then shunted past 'experiences'. Sometimes the ride is effortless and you aren't aware of the mechanisms. At other times long queues form and you are ushered into people pens. Multinationals, such as Pepsi, Ford, General Electric and Gulf, have heavily invested in Disney Enterprises.

continuously-rolling pleasure, the shunting of people into queues, pens and moving lines, a process which was perfected by Walt Disney, has now been applied to all areas of mass tourism, resulting in the controlled bland experience. What started as a search for adventure has ended in total predictability. Excessive growth and rationalism have contradicted the very goals that the institution of tourism and planned travel was set up to deliver.

The same is true of large architectural offices. Here design suffers because no one has control over the whole job from beginning to end, and because the building has to be produced quickly and efficiently according to proven formulae (the rationalisation of taste into clichés based on statistical averages of style and theme). Furthermore, with large buildings such as the Penta, the architecture has to be produced for a client whom no one in the office knows, (that is, the ten corporations), and who is, in any case, not the user of the building. In short, buildings today are nasty, brutal and too big because they are produced for profit by absentee developers, for absentee landlords for absent users whose taste is assumed as clichéd.

There is, then, not one cause of the crisis in architecture, but a *system of causes*; and clearly to change just the style or ideology of the architects, as is proposed by many critics, isn't going to change the whole situation. No amount of disaffection for the International Style or Brutalism, for high-rise, bureaucracy, capitalism, gigantism, or whatever else is the latest scapegoat is going to change things suddenly and produce a humane environment. It would seem we have to change the whole system of architectural production at once, all eleven causes together. And yet perhaps such a radical move is not necessary. Perhaps some causes are redundant, some are more important than others, and we only have to change a

15, 16 MIES VAN DER ROHE, *Seagram Building,* New York, 1958. Corner detail and plan. The plane of I-beams is extended out a few inches from the column line so that the corner is clearly articulated with angles of steel. The interior curtains now can only be raised to pre-selected, harmonious positions. Mies kept full-scale I-beam details by his desk to get the proportions just so. He thought this member was the modern equivalent of the Doric column, but as Herbert Read once said: 'In the back of every dying civilisation sticks a bloody Doric column'.

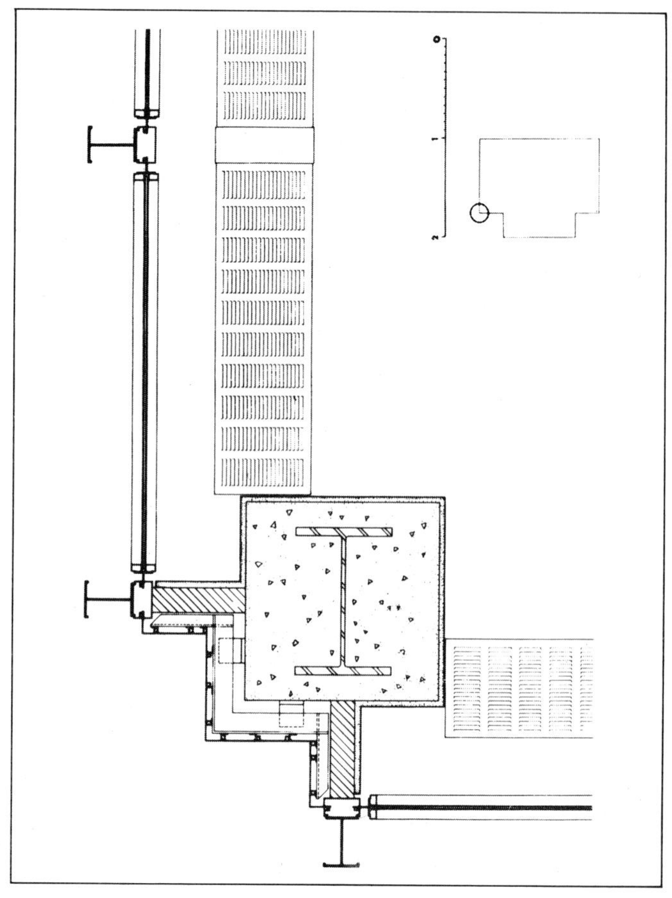

14 MIES VAN DER ROHE, *Lake Shore Drive Housing,* Chicago, 1950. The first classic use of the curtain wall sets the formula for further variations which Mies pursued to the end of his life. Here the black steel facade line is without depth and the curtains behind the glass are allowed a random setting – 'problems' which Mies later 'solved'. The greater problem, that housing looks like offices, was never raised. (John Winter).

combination of a few. For instance, if large architectural offices were divided into small teams, given a certain financial and design control, and put in close relation to the ultimate users of the building, this might be enough. Who knows? Experiments must be tried with different variables. All that can be said at this point is that the situation has systemic causes which have to be varied as a structure if deep changes are to be made. I will pursue only two causes of the crisis: the way the modern movement has impoverished architectural language on the level of form; and has itself suffered an impoverishment on the level of content, the social goals for which it actually built.

Univalent form

For the general aspect of an architecture created around one (or a few) simplified values, I will use the term **univalence**. No doubt in terms of expression the architecture of Mies van der Rohe and his followers is the most univalent formal system we have, because it makes use of few materials and a single, right-angled geometry. Characteristically this reduced style was justified as rational (when it was uneconomic), and universal (when it fitted only a few functions). The glass-and-steel-box has become the single most used form in modern architecture, and it signifies throughout the world 'office building'.

Yet in the hands of Mies and his disciples this impoverished system has become fetishised to the point where it overwhelms all other concerns (in a similar way the leather boot dominates the shoe fetishist and distracts him from larger concerns). Are I-beams and plate glass appropriate to housing? That is a question Mies would dismiss as irrelevant. The whole question of appropriateness, 'decorum', which every architect from Vitruvius to Lutyens debated, is now rendered obsolete by Mies' universal grammar and universal contempt for place and function. (He considered function as ephemeral, or so provisional as to be unimportant.)

14 His first, classic use of the curtain wall was on housing, not for an office – and obviously not for functional or communicational reasons, but because he was obsessed by perfecting certain formal problems. In this case, Mies concentrated on the proportion of the I-beam to panel,
15, set-back, glass area, supporting columns and articulating
16 lines. He kept full-scale details of these members close to his draughting board so he'd never lose sight of his loved ones.

A larger question thus didn't arise: what if housing looked like offices, or what if the two functions were indistinguishable? Clearly the net result would be to diminish and compromise both functions by equating them: working and living would become interchangeable on the most banal, literal level, and unarticulated on a higher, metaphorical plane. The psychic overtones to these two different activities would remain unexplored, accidental, truncated.

Another masterpiece of the modern movement, the
17 Chicago Civic Center, designed by a follower of Mies, also shows these confusions in communication. The long horizontal spans and dark corten steel express 'office building', 'power', 'purity', and the variations in surface express 'mechanical equipment'; but these primitive (and occasionally mistaken) meanings don't take us very far. On the most literal level the building does not communicate its important civic function; nor, more importantly, the social and psychological meanings of this very significant

17 C. F. MURPHEY, *Chicago Civic Center,* 1964. In terms of Mies' curtain wall this solution shows the horizontal emphasis – long spans and underplayed verticals in brown, especially rusted steel. Except for the Picasso sculpture out front, you would not recognise the civic importance of this building, nor the various political functions that occur within. (Hedrich-Blessing).

building task (a meeting place for the citizens of Chicago).

How could an architect justify such inarticulate building? The answer lies in terms of an ideology which celebrates process, which symbolises only the changes in technology and building material. The modern movement fetishised the means of production, and Mies, in one of those rare, cryptic aphorisms that is too hilarious, or rather delirious, to let pass, gave expression to this fetish.

> I see in industrialization the central problem of building in our time. If we succeed in carrying out this industrialization, the social, economic, technical, and also artistic problems will be readily solved. (1924)[1]

What about the theological and gastronomic 'problems'? The bizarre confusion to which this can lead is shown by Mies himself in the Illinois Institute of Technology campus in Chicago, a large enough collection of varied functions for us to regard it as a microcosm of his surrealist world.

Basically, he has used his universal grammar of steel I-beams along with an infill of beige brick and glass to speak about all the important functions: housing, assembly, classrooms, student union, shops, chapel, and so forth. If we look at a series of these buildings in turn we can see how confusing his language is, both literally and metaphorically.

A characteristic rectangular shape might be deciphered 18
as a teaching block where students churn out one similar idea after another on an assembly line – because the factory metaphor suggests this interpretation. The only

18 MIES VAN DER ROHE, *Siegel Building, IIT,* Chicago, 1947. Is this an astrophysical research lab? The whole campus is in the 'universal' aesthetic of steel, glass and beige brick, except for the most important building. (*See* 22).

19 THE INFAMOUS IIT CORNER of the previous building. The corner looked like a full *visual* stop to Leslie Martin, yet Llewelyn-Davies argued it looked 'endless' because it was stepped back with two I-beams and an L-beam. The fact that the whole building signified 'factory', when it was for teaching, was typically overlooked in this fetish for details and esoteric meaning.

20 MIES VAN DER ROHE, *IIT Cathedral/Boiler House,* Chicago, 1947. The traditional form of a basilica with central nave and two side aisles. There are even clerestory lights, a regular bay system and campanile to show that this is the cathedral.

recognisable sign in the building, the lattice-work disc at the top, suggests that the students are budding astro-physicists; but of course Mies cannot claim credit for this bit of literalism. Someone else added it, destroying the purity of his fundamental utterance. What he can claim credit for, and what has exercised great architectural debate, (a debate between two English deans, Sir Leslie Martin and Lord Llewelyn-Davies), is his solving of the
19 *problem* of the corner. These two schoolmen disputed, with medieval precision and inconsequentiality, whether the corner symbolised 'endlessness', or 'closedness' like a Renaissance pilaster. The fact that it could symbolise both or neither, depending on the code of the viewer, or the fact that larger questions of factory symbolism and semantic confusion were at stake – such questions were never raised.

Not so far away from this disputatious corner is another architectural conundrum, designed in Mies' universal 20
language of confusion. Here we can see all sorts of conventional cues which give the game away: a rectangular form of cathedral, a central nave structure with two side aisles expressed in the eastern front. The religious nature of this building is heightened by a regular bay system of piers; it's true there are no pointed arches, but there are

21 MIES VAN DER ROHE, *IIT Boiler House/Church.* A dumb box placed to either side of high-rise buildings, which are in the same vernacular. Blank on three sides and lit by a search light – clearly this is the boiler house.

22 MIES VAN DER ROHE, *IIT President's Temple/School of Architecture,* Chicago, 1962. The black temple hovers miraculously from a giant order of steel trusses and a minor order of I-beams. The white horizontal steps also break the law of gravity. The building occupies a major point on the campus, as the President's house should. (John Winter).

clerestory windows on both aisle and nave elevations. Finally, to confirm our reading that this *is* the campus cathedral, we see the brick campanile, the bell tower that dominates the basilica.

In fact, this is the boiler house, a solecism of such stunning wit that it can't be truly appreciated until we see
21 the actual chapel, which looks like a boiler house. This is an unassuming box in industrial materials, sandwiched balefully between dormitory slabs with a searchlight attached – in short, signs which confirm a reading of prosaic utility.

Finally, we come to the most important position on campus, the central area, where there is a temple constructed in a homogeneous material that distinguishes it from the other factories. This temple is raised on a plinth, 22
it has a magnificent colonnade of major and minor orders, and a grandiose stairway of white marble planes miraculously hovering in space, as if the local god has ultimately worked his magic. It must be the President's house, or at very least, the Administration Centre. Actually it's where the architects work – what else could it be?

So we see the factory is a classroom, the cathedral is a boiler house, the boiler house is a chapel, and the President's temple is the School of Architecture. Thus

23 FRANK LLOYD WRIGHT, *Marin County Civic Center,* San Rafael, California, 1959–64. The great *Pont du Gard* made out of cardboard, gilt and golden bauble, surmounted by an Aztec minaret, with interior bowling-alleys of space, and a baby-blue, opaline roof with cookie-cutter hemi-circles. An excellent piece of Kitsch modern, unfortunately unintended.

24 I. M. PEI, *Everson Museum,* Syracuse, New York, 1968. Hardly communicative as a museum. It might be a warehouse, four theatres, or a church, except that the blank box with funny shapes became *the* sign of museums in America by 1975. By stressing sculptural consistency above all other values, Pei's work becomes surreal and reduced in significance.

25 I. M. PEI, *Christian Science Church Center,* Boston, 1973. Very hard-edge Le Corbusier – in fact Chandigarh done with precision concrete. From the air you can appreciate the fact that this centre is laid out like a giant phallus which culminates, appropriately, in a fountain. Ledoux designed a phallus-planned building as a brothel, but there is no further indication here that some elaborate message is intended.

Mies is saying that the boiler house is more important than the chapel, and that architects rule, as pagan gods, over the lot. Of course Mies didn't intend these propositions, but his commitment to reductive formal values inadvertently betrays them.

Univalent formalists and inadvertent symbolists

Lest we think Mies is a special case, or somehow uncharacteristic of modern architects in general, let us look at similar examples which stem from the reaction against his particular language: the formalist reaction in America and the Team Ten critique in Europe both turned against the Miesian approach in the sixties.

23 Frank Lloyd Wright's last work, the Marin County Civic Center, is characteristic of the formalist architecture. The building is based on the endless repetition of various patterns (and their transformation), which are uncertain in their overtones – in this case the baby-blue and golden baubles reminiscent of a Helena Rubenstein ambience, and superimposed arches associated with a Roman aqueduct. The arches belie their compression function and hang, with gilded struts, in tension. A golden minaret-totem-pole, which also has Aztec and Mayan associations, crowns the site of this city centre (which is missing only its city). In defence one can applaud its compelling, surrealist image, justifiable in terms of its kitsch extravagance, but not much more. Like the Chicago Civic Center already mentioned, it doesn't tell us anything very profound about the role of government (escapism?) or the citizens' relation to it.

If we look at the work of I. M. Pei, Ulrich Franzen, 24,
Philip Johnson or Skidmore, Owings and Merrill, the 25,
leading American architects, we find the same erratic 26
signification – always a striking form, a reduced but potent image, with unintended meanings. For instance, Gordon Bunshaft's museum for the Hirschhorn Collection,

26 SKIDMORE, OWINGS and MERRILL, Bunshaft designer, *Bieneke Library,* Yale University, 1964. This pompous temple looks extraordinary at night when the light shines through the translucent marble: the panels look like stacked television sets which have all gone on the blink. (US Information Service).

27 GORDON BUNSHAFT and SOM, *Hirschhorn Museum,* Washington DC, 1973. Symbolism at its most inadvertent – a concrete pillbox meant to protect art from the people? A marble doughnut? (Hirshhorn Museum).

the only collection of modern art on the Mall in Washington, is in the very powerful form of a white masonry
27 cylinder. This simplified shape, ultimately stemming from the eighteenth-century 'modernists', Boullée and Ledoux, was meant to communicate power, awe, harmony and the sublime. And so it does. But, as *Time* magazine and other journals pointed out, it symbolises more accurately a concrete bunker, a Normandy pillbox, with its battered walls, impenetrable heaviness, and 360 degree machine-gun slit. Bunshaft is inadvertently saying 'keep modern art from the public in this fortified stronghold and shoot 'em down if they dare approach'. So many cues, in such a popular code, reinforce this meaning and make it obvious to everyone not retrained in the architects' code. It might have been a multivalent statement of this meaning had the architect really intended it and combined the pillbox image with further cues of an ironic nature. But, as with the unintended witticisms of Mrs Malaprop, all credit for humour must go to the subconscious.

Aldo Rossi and the Italian Rationalists try very sympa-
28, 29 thetically to continue the classical patterns of Italian cities, designing neutral buildings which have a 'zero degree' of historical association; but their work invariably recalls the Fascist architecture of the thirties – despite countless disclaimers. The semantic overtones are again erratic, and focus on such oppressive meanings, because the building is oversimplified and monotonous. Serious critics and apologists for them, such as Manfredo Tafuri, find themselves evading the obvious in their attempt to justify such buildings with elaborate, esoteric interpretation.[2]

28 ALDO ROSSI, *The Gallaratese Neighbourhood,* Milan, 1969–71. A long portico of repeated piers is surmounted by endlessly recurring rectangular windows. The interior corridors are also barren funnels of emptiness. Because the forms are 'empty' some critics have assumed they are above historical associations; but the signs are conventional and the meanings are quite well established in Italy.

29 GUERRINI, LAPADULA and ROMANO, *Palace of Italian Civilisation, Eur,* Rome, 1942. Deflowered classicism and endlessly repeated blank forms. This is the architecture of control, and some future study may show how it depends on boring redundancy for its coercion.

30 HERMAN HERTZBERGER, *Old Age Home,* Amsterdam, 1975. An intricate puzzle of small-scaled elements, a human scale in the details. But this is multiplied to vast proportions. The incessant symbolism of white crosses containing black coffins is equally unpremeditated and unfortunate.

This disparity between popular and elitist codes can be
found everywhere in the modern movement, especially 31
among the most highly acclaimed architects, such as
James Stirling, Arata Isozaki, Ricardo Bofill and Herman 74
Hertzberger. The better the modern architect, the less he 30
can control obvious meanings. Hertzberger's Old Age Home is, on a sophisticated level, the delightful casbah he intended, with many small-scale places and a closely-grained urban fabric where the individual is psychologically hidden and protected by the nooks and crannies. As an abstract piece of form it communicates humanism, care, intricacy and delicacy. That is the Chinese puzzle quality of the various interlocked elements and spaces acquire these meanings by analogy. Yet such subtle analogy is hardly enough when more potent, metaphorical meanings have run amok. For what are the obvious associations of this Old Age Home? Each room looks like a black coffin placed between white crosses (in fact a veritable war cemetery of white crosses). Despite his humanism, the architect is inadvertently saying that old age, in our society, is rather fatal.

Ah well, these 'slips-of-the-metaphor' are committed more and more by the top modernists, and they can even be made by architects who see architecture as a language – by Peter and Alison Smithson. It is interesting that, like other apologists for the modern movement since 1850, they justify their work in terms of the linguistic analogy,

31 ARATA ISOZAKI, *Gunma Prefectural Museum,* Takasaki, 1974. A dramatic sequence of spaces is disciplined by aluminium squares and grids everywhere. But the technocratic overtones are unsympathetic to certain kinds of fine art exhibited inside, and the overall expression is limited to a single range of meanings: precision, order, and the pervasive hospital metaphor so common in modern architecture. (Masao Arai/Japan Architect).

and look to previous languages of architecture for their lesson. They say of the city of Bath: 'it's unique . . . for its remarkable cohesion, *for a form language understood by all . . . contributed by all*'.[3] Their analysis of this Georgian city of light and dark stonework shows it to have a wide relevant language, a consistent language, from humble
32 details such as street grills, to grand gestures such as porticoes. These porticoes the Smithsons characterise as **metaphors** for large doors, and pediments as metaphors for cheaper doors – in short, they are acutely aware of the way architectural language depends on *traditional* symbolism.

This makes their own anti-traditionalism all the more poignant and bizarre; but the Smithsons, as veritable descendants of the Romantic Age, must 'make it new' each time to avoid the censure of conventionality. Thereby, of course, they successfully avoid communicating, for all developed languages must contain a high degree of conventional usage, if only to make innovations and deviations from the norm more correctly understood.

When speaking about a possible modern language, Peter Smithson comes down firmly like a 1920s modernist in support of a machine aesthetic.

> . . . for the machine-supported present-day cities, only a live, cool, highly controlled, rather impersonal architectural language can deepen that base-connection, make it resonate with culture as a whole.[4]

The fallacies of this position are well known, yet many architects today are still committed to such notions because of their training in processes of production, and their ideology of progress. They still believe in a *Zeitgeist*, and one determined by machinery and technology – so the buildings they produce symbolise these now somewhat old-fashioned demons.

The great irony is, however, that they also believe in providing essentially humanist values of 'place, identity,

32 JOHN WOOD II, *Royal Crescent,* Bath, 1767–80. One of the first examples of housing treated as a palace – the coliseum was another model. Although making a grand urban gesture, the individual houses still have an identity, marked by vertical separation and several variations in articulation (chimneys, fire walls, fences). The Smithsons are acutely aware of this symbolism, which makes their failure to provide its equivalent all the more poignant. (Bath City Council).

33 ALISON and PETER SMITHSON, *Robin Hood Gardens,* London, 1968–72. Unrelieved concrete (except for curtains), popularly identified now with the image of an industrial *process*. The variations of vertical fins are not strong enough to identify each apartment. The packed-in scale gives the feeling of there being a dense human wall.

personality, home-coming', (I am quoting from several Team Ten sources, values which the Smithsons share). How can you communicate these meanings if you use a new language based on the machine metaphor? It would be very hard, practically impossible, and the Smithsons haven't yet pulled off this miracle. Their Robin Hood
33 Gardens, in the East End of London, simply does not do the trick.

Robin Hood Gardens is not a modern version of the Bath Crescent, in spite of the large urban gesture and V-shaped plan. It does not accentuate the identity of each house, although Smithson admires Bath for being 'unmistakably a collection of separate houses'. It suppresses this in favour of visual syncopation, a partially randomised set of vertical fins, and horizontal continuity – the notion of a communal street deck. These 'streets in the air' have, surprisingly, all the faults which the Smithsons had
34 recognised in other similar schemes. They are under-used;
35 the collective entries are paltry and a few have been vandalised. Indeed, they are dark, smelly, dank passageways. Little sense of place, few collective facilities and fewer 'identifying elements', which the architects had reasonably said were needed in modern buildings.

34, 35 SMITHSONS, *Robin Hood Gardens,* street in the air, and collective entry. The long empty streets in the air don't have the life or facilities of the traditional street. The entry ways, one of which has been burned, are dark and anonymous, serving too many families. The scheme has many of the problems which Oscar Newman traced to a lack of defensible space. Here architectural critic Paul Goldberger mimes an act that often occurs.

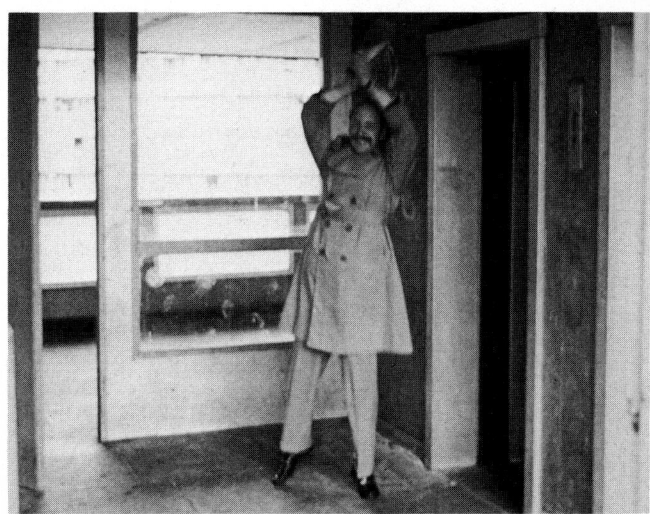

36, 37 LAS VEGAS and EXETER CATHEDRAL CLOSE, two different kinds of social manifestations in which the architecture lends itself to direct symbolic expression. Regardless of our views of either social group, it has to be said that modern architects have disregarded this level of symbolic detail and particularity. Most cities contain ethnic diversity, but what large development incorporates the Chinese restaurant, the front of the local butcher? Architects have been too removed from this level of detail, and will be until they are retrained as anthropologists or journalists to understand social reality.

The Smithsons claim they have provided a sense of place.

> On the garden side the building is unified. It is an urban place, a part of the definition of a city, provided it does not become a repetitive pattern which organizes an homogeneous space.[5]

Indeed the space isn't homogeneous, it has kinks and an artificial mound near the centre. But these deviations from the norm and the subtle cues of visual separation are hardly strong enough to override the repetitive pattern and homogeneous material. These signify more strongly 'council housing', 'anonymity', 'the authorities didn't have enough money to use wood, stucco, etc.' – in short, they signify 'social deprivation'. The Smithsons' laudable intentions of providing a community building on the scale of the Bath Crescent and offering the same degree of individual expression and identity in an architectural language understood by all – these positive aims are denied by the built form.

Such contradictions between statement and result have reached impressive proportions in modern architecture, and one can now speak of a 'credibility gap' that parallels the loss of trust in politicians. The root causes of this are, I believe, based on the nature of architecture as a language. It is *radically schizophrenic* by necessity, partly rooted in tradition, in the past – indeed in everyone's childhood experience of crawling around on flat floors and perceiving such normal architectural elements as vertical doors. And it is partly rooted in a fast-changing society, with its new functional tasks, new materials, new technologies and ideologies. On the one hand, architecture is as slow-changing as spoken language (we can still understand Renaissance English); and, on the other, as fast-changing and esoteric as modern art and science.

Put another way, we learn from the beginning the cultural signs which make any urban place particular to a social group, an economic class and real, historical people; whereas modern architects spend their time unlearning all these particular signs in an attempt to design for universal man, or Mythic Modern Man. This

EXETER CATHEDRAL CLOSE

3-M monster of course doesn't exist, except as a historical fiction – the creation of modern novelists, sociologists and idealistic planners. Mr Triple-M is no doubt a logical necessity for architects and others who want to generalise a statistical average. Tom Wolfe has criticised novelists for writing about such non-existing creatures, and the same points could be scored against architects.[6] They try to provide modern man with a mythic consciousness, with consistent patterns reminiscent of tribal societies, refined in their purity, full of tasteful 'unity in variety', and other such geometric harmonies; when in fact modern man doesn't exist, and what he would want if he did perchance
6, 37 exist would be realistic social signs. Signs of status, history, commerce, comfort, ethnic domain, signs of being neighbourly, (though also a bit better off than the Joneses). Modern architects aren't trained in these codes, they don't know how to get close to this reality, and so they go on providing a mythic integration of community, (often now a projection of middle-class values).

Too bad: society can go on without architects, personalise its housing estates or blow them up, or hire interior decorators. It doesn't matter (except in Russia); there are always other realistic professions who are ready to move in.

In any case, before we finish with this modern architecture-bashing (a form of sadism which is getting far too easy), we should mention one dilemma architects face, (which isn't entirely of their own making), because it has an effect on the language they use.

Univalent content

Let us now examine the major commissions, the most prevalent building types which have engaged the skill of architects in this century. A certain disinterest is needed here, because the truths are hard and the solutions not forthcoming. Many will deny or gloss over the social realities behind architecture because they are so trivial and depressing and of no one's desire, no one's fault. The major mistake architects made in this century, on this score, is perhaps to have been born at all.

Let us look anyway at the major monuments of modern architecture and the social tasks for which they were built. Here we will find a strange but unnoticed deflection of the modern architect's *role as a social utopian*, for we will see that he has actually built for the reigning powers of an established, commercial society; and this surreptitious liaison has taken its toll, as illicit love affairs will. The modern movement of architecture, conceived in the 1850s as a call to morality, and in the 1920s (in its Heroic Period) as a call to social transformation, found itself unwittingly compromised, first by practice and then by acceptance.[7] These architects wished to give up their subservient role as 'tailors' to society and what they regarded as 'a corrupt ruling taste', and become instead 'doctors', leaders, prophets, or at least midwives, to a new social order. But for what order did they build?

1 **Monopolies and big business.** Some of the accepted classics of modern architecture were built for clients who today are multinational corporations. Peter
38 Behrens' Berlin Turbine Factory was for the General
Electric of its day, AEG. This building of 1909 is often considered the first great work of European modern architecture because of its pure volumetric expression, its clear clean use of glass and steel, almost the curtain wall, and its refinement of utilitarian products – the beginning of industrial design. Further landmarks of architecture, those that modified the language slightly, were Frank
Lloyd Wright's curvilinear poetry of pyrex tubing and 39
streamlined brick, built for a large wax company; Gordon Bunshaft's classic solution for the office tower, two pure slabs set at right angles, one on top of the other, erected
for the multinational based on soap; Mies van der Rohe's 40
dark, Rolls-Royce solution to the curtain wall built for the Seagram's Whiskey giant; Eero Saarinen's walk-
through bird-of-prey built for TWA; and numerous refine- 69
ments of the curtain wall built by the large offices, such as Skidmore, Owings and Merrill, for soft drink companies, tobacco chains, international banks and oil companies. How should one express the power and concentration of capital, the mercantile function, the exploitation of markets? These building tasks would be the monuments of our time, because they bring in the extra money for architecture; and yet their potential role as social paragons is without credibility.

38 PETER BEHRENS, *AEG Factory*, Berlin, 1909. Often regarded as one of the first great modern buildings, the fountainhead too of industrial design, this work set the factory as the major metaphor for subsequent building. Here the marriage was made between big business, 'good design', and the functional style. This union was eagerly sought for at the time by the German *Werkbund*, and it bore multi-national fruit sixty years later. (Bauhaus Archive).

39 FRANK LLOYD WRIGHT, *Johnson Wax Building*, Racine, Wisconsin, 1938. Columns taper downwards and are supported on brass shoes. Everything takes up the curve theme in this 'total work of art'. The idea of a unified corporate image became standard by the fifties for such multinationals as the CBS, IBM, Olivetti, etc. (US Information Service).

Opposite
40 GORDON BUNSHAFT and SOM, *Lever Brothers Building*, New York City, 1951–2. The first convincing use of the light curtain wall. Spandrels and glass alternate in horizontal bands which are then covered by a neutral mesh of mullions. By the sixties, many multinationals on Park Avenue had similar corporate boxes.

41 JOHN KIBBLE, *Glasgow Botanic Garden,* 1873. Recreated from a former building as 'the Crystal Art Palace', this glasshouse recalls Indian architecture and onion domes. The large squashed dome at the back is 146ft across, and had at its centre a lilypond in which an orchestra played: the ceiling opened and closed for diminuendo and crescendo. (Easter Young).

2 **International exhibitions, World Fairs.** Another geneology of modern architecture is traced from the
41, 42 Crystal Palace of 1851 to the Theme Pavilion at Osaka 1970. This line of descent has a series of technical triumphs to its credit, resulting in the new language of lattice structures, the open girders of Eiffel, the pin-jointed parabolas of industrial sheds, the translucent and geometric domes of Buckminster Fuller, and the soaring tents of Frei Otto (these tents always soar in architectural criticism). Indeed these triumphs did a great deal to aestheticise the experience of architecture: historians and critics skipped lightly over the content of the structures, their propagandist role; and focused instead on their spatial and optical qualities. The mass media followed suit. Overlooked was the blatant nationalism and ersatz
43 ambience which constituted ninety per cent of the World Fairs. Why? Because this ignored content was so obviously hedonistic and lacking in subtlety, and because there was no great understanding of how this blatant content works in mass culture, nor how it is occasionally humorous, creative and provocative.

Opposite above
42 KENZO TANGE, *Theme Pavilion, EXPO 70,* Osaka, 1970. A megastructure carrying various services was finally built after being contemplated by the avant-garde for ten years. World Fairs often allow such grandiose and creative ideas to be realised, and have therefore played an important role in the evolution of modern architecture. (Masao Arai).

Opposite below
43 The CAMBODIAN PAVILION, Osaka, 1970. Designed with the advice of Prince Norodom Sihanouk, this typically nationalist pavilion echoes Khmer architecture and Angkor Vat. Most World's Fair architecture has an air of pastiche about it which could offend convinced nationalists, but it conforms to mass standards of propriety. This manifestation is overlooked by serious critics and remains undiscussed. (Japan Information Service).

44 PATRICK HODGKINSON, *Foundling Estate,* London, 1973. Long lines of housing with greenhouse living-rooms are stacked on the diagonal. The grand public entrance, the largest of its kind in Great Britain, looks as if it leads to a ceremonial space, at least a stadium, but it actually culminates in an empty plaza. The Futurist styling and semantic confusion are again a consequence of the modern movement's rejection of rhetoric and a theory of communication.

Below
45 RICHARD ROGERS and RENZO PIANO, *Pompidou Centre,* Paris, 1977. Gigantic trusses manufactured by Krupp and brought through Paris streets early in the morning, hold up this spiky cultural centre. The technological image is carried through with conviction, especially on the services which are painted in strong primary colours. By sinking the building and breaking up its facade, the scale is sympathetic with the traditional Paris street pattern. (Bernard Vincent).

3 **Factories and engineering feats.** From Walter Gropius' Fagus Factory, 1911, to Le Corbusier's 'home as a machine for living in', 1922, we have the birth and establishment of the major metaphor for modern architecture: the factory. Housing was conceived in this image, and the Nazis were not altogether wrong in attacking the first international manifesto of this metaphor, the *Weissenhof Siedlungen*, 1927, for its inappropriateness. Why should houses adopt the imagery of the mass production
44 line and the white purity of the hospital?

More recent mass housing in England, for instance that
46 in London, or Milton Keynes, has followed this pervasive twentieth-century metaphor. That no one asked to live in a factory did not occur to the doctor-modern-architect, because he was out to cure the disease of modern cities, no matter how distasteful the medicine. Indeed, better if it tasted like castor oil and caused convulsions, because then the transformation of bourgeois society was more likely to be complete, the patient would reform his petty acquisitive drives and become a good collectivised citizen.

Such metaphors for housing have been rejected almost everywhere they've been applied, (exceptions occur in Germany and Switzerland), but they have taken hold in appropriate areas: stadia, sports grounds, aircraft hangars,
, 47 and all the large-span structures traditionally associated with engineering. Here the poetry of process is exhilarating

46 JEREMY DIXON, CHRIS CROSS and ED JONES, *'Netherfield' Milton Keynes Housing,* 1974. Another long line, now accentuated by structural fins and a flat roof plane, is the apotheosis of the assembly-line metaphor applied to housing. (John Donat).

47 KENZO TANGE, *National Gymnasia for the Olympic Games,* Tokyo, 1964. Two buildings in subtle counterpoint are placed on a podium. The concrete masts, which hold the hyperbolic curves, end in the typical Japanese 'slant' which has become something of a cliché. The gentle curves and structural expression are also traditional signs.

without being wildly inappropriate or surreal, and we can claim the single, unmitigated triumph of modern architecture on the level of content.

4 **Consumer temples and churches of distraction.** Someone from an alien culture would be amazed to see, if he took a quick helicopter trip over any of our sprawling cities, that urban man worshipped at institutions devoted to commercial gods. Modern architects haven't altogether mastered this territory of Disneyland and ride-through parks, of Kings Road and Sunset Strip, but they are beginning to try, and we can already count the triumphs. The exquisite technological jewels of Hans Hollein, the 48-5
boutiques and candle shops, and high-gloss mausolea given over to selling religious relics for the wedding finger. So much design talent and mystery expended on such small shops would convince an outsider that he had at last stumbled on the true faith of this civilisation. And when he came to see the same medals worshipped in the

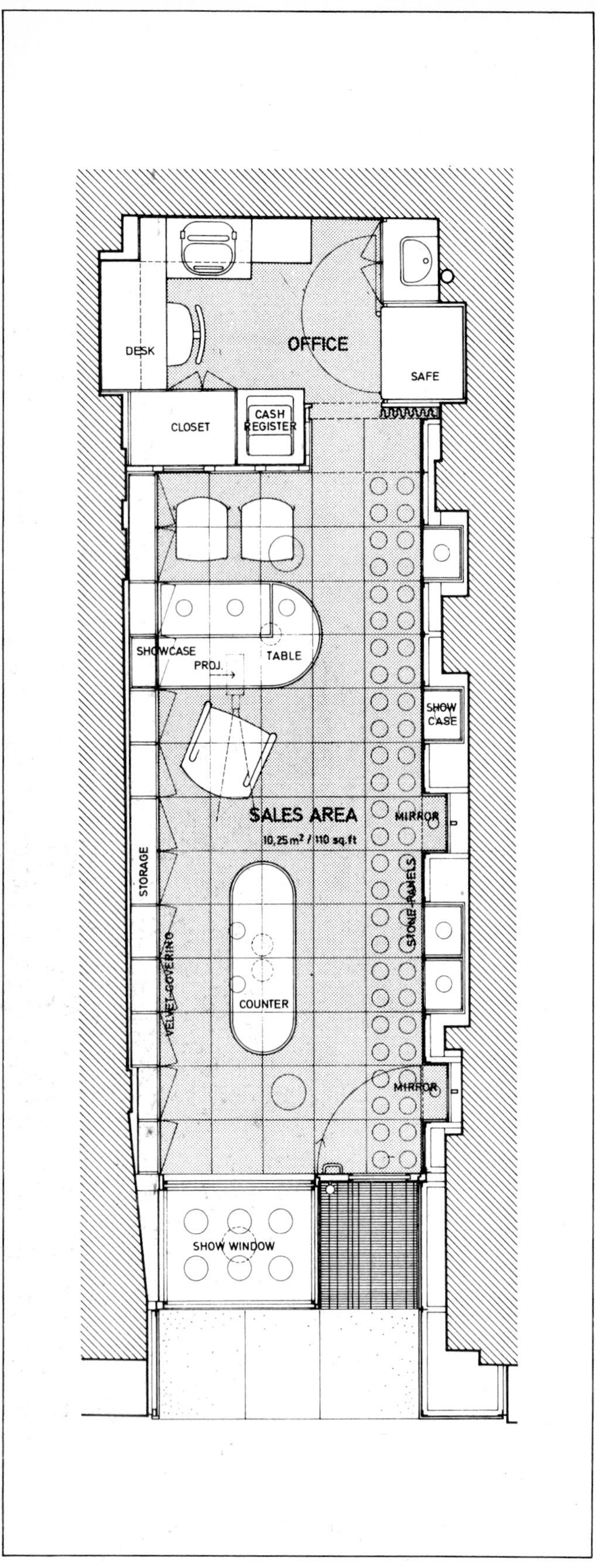

48, 49 HANS HOLLEIN, *Jewellery Shop,* Vienna, 1975. Hollein uses voluptuous, shiny marble to set off the polished mechanical equipment. The contrast of circle and fissure, of skin-like marble and the glistening gold lips folding over each other, is explicitly ironic and sexual. Tight space is ingeniously cut up to loosen the customer's libido even further. Perhaps only a Viennese could have brought off this mixture of commerce and sensuality. (Jerzy Surwillo).

50 HANS HOLLEIN, *Jewellery Shop,* Vienna, 1975.

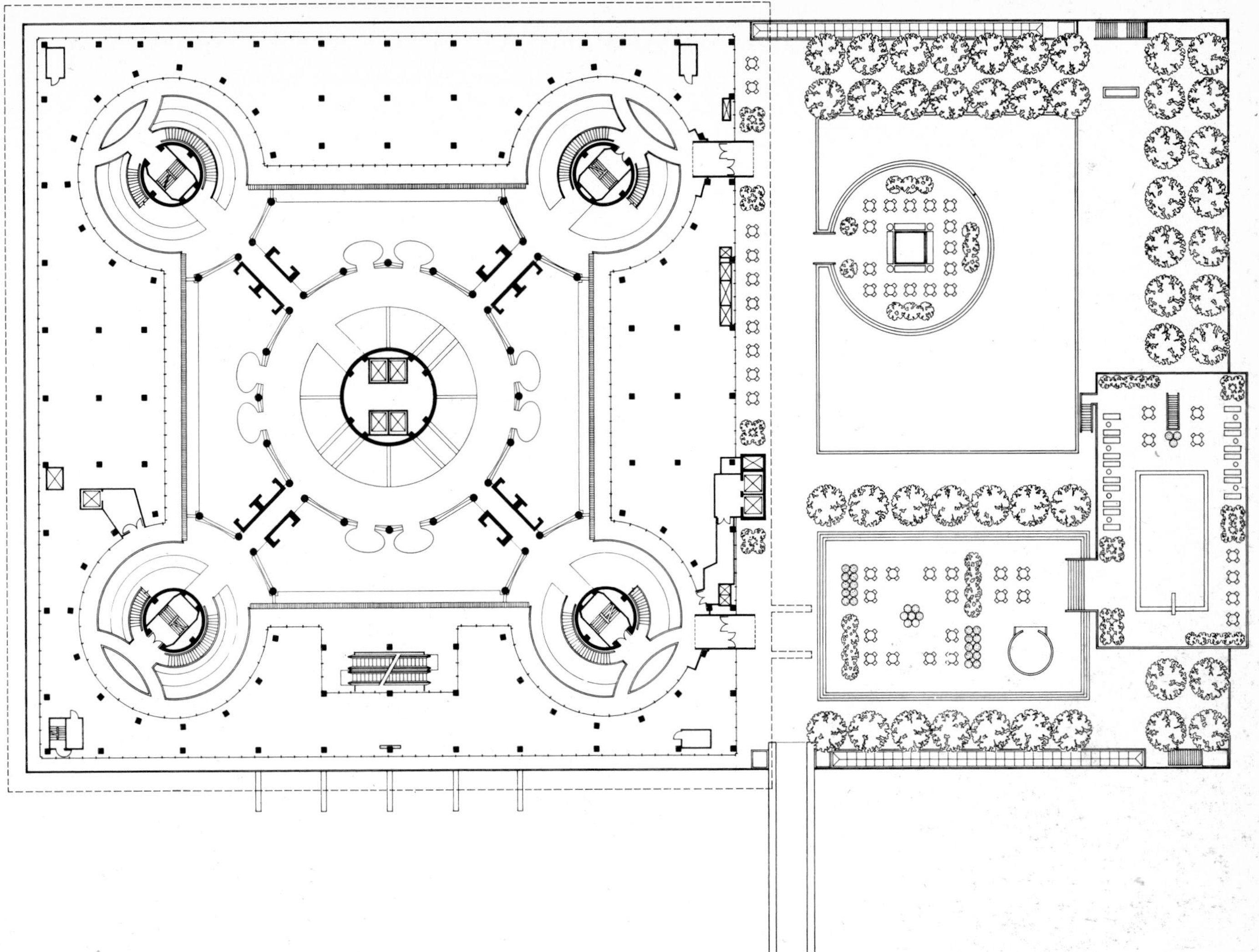

51, 52 JOHN PORTMAN, *Bonaventure Hotel*, model, Los Angeles, 1976. Portman has revived the nineteenth-century tradition of the grand hotel – at least the cost part of this tradition – with his lavish Regency Hyatts in several American cities. He gives the exteriors an absolute geometric image, parts of which in mirrorplate reflect like overblown jewels. The planning is reminiscent of the megalomaniacal schemes of Boullée.

large hotels, constructed in the theological material of
51 mirrorplate, his interpretation would be confirmed. The culture idolises tinsel, personal adornment, private jewellery. The more adept modern architects become at embellishing buildings (and of course they are working at a distinct disadvantage, having previously equated 'ornament' and 'crime'), the more the anomaly appears. A jewel is a jewel, is not a fitting object for great architecture. The banality of content will not go away.

Architecture obviously reflects what a society holds important, what it values both spiritually and in terms of cash. In the pre-industrial past the major areas for expression were the temple, the church, the palace, agora, meeting house, country house and city hall; while in the present, extra money is spent on hotels, restaurants and all those commercial building types I have mentioned. Public housing and buildings expressing the local community or the public realm receive the cutbacks. Buildings representing consumer values generate the investment. As Galbraith says of American capitalism, it results in private wealth and public squalor.

Several modern architects, in a desperate attempt to cheer themselves up, have decided that since this is an inevitable situation, it must also have its good points. Commercial tasks are more democratic than the previous aristocratic and religious ones; 'Main Street is almost all right' according to Robert Venturi.

When these commercial design tasks first emerged into consciousness, about the turn of this century, they were celebrated by the Futurist, Sant' Elia, with a glee and moralising tone that were later to become common. He contrasted the new building tasks, given over to commerce and energy, with the previous ones devoted to worship – the nineteenth-century dynamo versus the thirteenth-century Virgin.

> The formidable antithesis between the modern world and the old is determined by all those things that formerly did not exist . . . we have lost our predilection for the monumental, the heavy, the static, and we have enriched our sensibility with a *taste for the light, the practical, the ephemeral and the swift*. We no longer feel ourselves to be the men of the cathedrals, the palaces and the tribunes. We are the men of the great

53 LAS VEGAS LIGHTSCAPE. The secular and commercial activities celebrated by the Futurists are realised here with a technological artistry they would have relished, but a social content on which they would have choked.

54 LITTLE CHAPEL of the FLOWERS, Las Vegas, 1960. Drive-in marriage and divorce, your Olde New England clapboard church advertised in neon, with totally automated services – a combination which is far too new and old at the same time, but one which appeals to vast numbers in a consumer society.

> hotels, the railway stations, the immense streets, colossal ports, covered markets, luminous arcades, straight roads and beneficial demolitions.[8]

In short, these embrace the social activities of a middle-class tourist wandering from railway station to hotel along wide super-highways dotted with bulldozed sites and lit by sparkling neon signs. With slight modifications, Sant'
53 Elia could be describing the glitter of Las Vegas, or less fashionably, let us say, the main street of Warsaw. Whatever the country, whatever the economic system, such secular building tasks are the important ones today, and so much modern art and architecture tries to celebrate this fact. 'The heroism of everyday life', that notion shared by Picasso, Léger and Le Corbusier in the twenties, was a philosophy which tried to place banal objects on a pedestal formerly reserved for special symbols of veneration. The fountain pen, the filing cabinet, the steel girder and the typewriter were the new icons. Mayakovsky and the Russian Constructivists took art into the streets and even performed one grand symphony of sirens and steam whistles, while waving coloured flags on top of factory roofs. The hope of these artists and architects was to reform society on a new class and functional basis: substitute power stations for cathedrals, technocrats for aristocrats. A new, heroic, democratic society would emerge, led by a powerful race of pagan supermen, the avant-garde, the technicians and captains of industry, the enlightened scientists and teams of experts. What a dream!

Indeed, the managerial revolution did occur, and socialist revolutions happened in a few countries; but the dream was taken over by Madison Avenue (and its equivalents), and the 'heroic object of everyday use' became the 'new, revolutionary detergent'. Societies kept on worshipping at their old altars, with diminishing faith, and tried to incorporate the new values at the same time.
The result? Ersatz culture, a caricature of the past and 54
future at once, a surreal fantasy dreamed up neither by the avant-garde, nor the traditionalists, and abhorrent to both of them.

With the triumph of consumer society in the West and bureaucratic State Capitalism in the East, our unfortunate modern architect was left without much uplifting social content to symbolise. If architecture has to concentrate its efforts on symbolising a way of life and the public realm, then it's in a bit of a fix when these things lose their credibility. There's nothing much the architect can do about this except protest as a citizen, and design dissenting buildings that express the complex situation. He can communicate the values which are missing and ironically criticise the ones he dislikes. But to do that he must make use of the language of the local culture, otherwise his message falls on deaf ears, or is distorted to fit this local language.

55 ADOLF LOOS, *Chicago Tribune Column.*

PART TWO
The Modes of Architectural Communication

Monsieur Jourdain, Molière's *Bourgeois Gentilhomme*,
was rather surprised to discover that he had been speaking
prose for forty years – 'without knowing anything about it'.
Modern architects might suffer a similar shock, or doubt
that they've been speaking anything as elevated as
prose. To look at the environment is to agree with their
56 doubt. We see a babble of tongues, a free-for-all of personal idiolects, not the classical language of the Doric,
Ionic and Corinthian Orders. Where there once were rules
of architectural grammar, we now have a mutual diatribe
between speculative builders; where there once was a
gentle discourse between the Houses of Parliament and
Westminster Abbey, there is now across the Thames, the
Shell Building shouting at the Hayward Gallery, which
57 grunts back at a stammering and giggling Festival Hall.
It's all confusion and strife, and yet this invective is still
language even if it's not very comprehensible or per-
suading. There *are* various analogies architecture shares
with language and if we use the terms loosely, we can
speak of architectural 'words', 'phrases', 'syntax', and
'semantics'. I will discuss several of these analogies in
turn, showing how they can be more consciously used as
communicational means, starting with the mode most
commonly disregarded in modern architecture.

Below
56 SAN FRANCISCO CITYSCAPE, 1973. With various skyscrapers, including a trussed rectangle and the triangular building, known affectionately as 'Pereiras' Prick' (he designed the Transamerican Corporation).

Below
57 The SOUTH BANK, London, 1976. With large chunks devoted to different functions: *left to right:* The Queen Elizabeth Hall, Royal Festival Hall and Shell Tower carry on their distinctive form of garbled conversation. Each chunk sends out a single, if muted, message that it is an 'important' monument of some unspecified kind.

Metaphor

People invariably see one building in terms of another, or in terms of a similar object; in short as a metaphor. The more unfamiliar a modern building is, the more they will compare it metaphorically to what they know. This matching of one experience to another is a property of all thought, particularly that which is creative. Thus when pre-cast concrete grills were first used on buildings in the late fifties, they were seen as 'cheesegraters', 'beehives', 'chain-link fences'; while ten years later when they became the norm in a certain building type, they were seen
58 in functional terms: 'this looks like a parking garage'. From metaphor to cliché, from neologism through constant usage to architectural **sign**, this is the continual route travelled by new and successful forms and technics.

Typical negative metaphors used by the public and by critics such as Lewis Mumford to condemn modern architecture were 'cardboard box', 'shoe-box', 'egg-crate', 'filing cabinet', 'grid-paper'. These comparisons were sought not only for their pejorative, mechanistic overtones, but also because they were strongly **coded** in a culture which had become sensitised to the spectre of 1984. This obvious point has some curious implications, as we shall see.

One implication became apparent when I was visiting Japan and the architect Kisho Kurokawa. We went to see
his new apartment tower in Tokyo, made from stacked 59
shipping containers, which had a most unusual overall shape. They looked like stacked sugar cubes, or even more, like superimposed washing machines, because the white cubes all had round windows in their centres. When I said this metaphor had unfortunate overtones for living, Kurokawa evinced suprise. 'They aren't washing machines, they're bird cages. You see in Japan we build concrete-box bird nests with round holes and place them in the trees. I've built these bird nests for itinerant businessmen who visit Tokyo, for bachelors who fly in every so often with their birds.' A witty answer, perhaps made up on the spot, but one which underscored very nicely a difference in our visual codes.

Left
58 CONCRETE GRILLS, now the sign of parking garage, were first used on offices in America in the late fifties. They work here to carry the external loads and mask the cars. While the 'cheesegrater' is now no longer perceived as a metaphor, the precast grill is on rare occasions still used for offices. Whether it signifies garage or office depends on the frequency of usage within a society.

Opposite
59 KISHO KUROKAWA, *Nakagin Capsule Building,* Tokyo, 1972. 140 boxes were driven to the site and lifted onto the two concrete cores. Each habitable room has built-in bathroom, stereo-tape deck, calculators and other amenities for the businessman. The metaphor of stacking rooms like bricks or sugar cubes has re-emerged every five years or so, since Walter Gropius proposed it in 1922. The overtones of this are ambiguous: to some they have always suggested regimentation, to others the unity in variety of the Italian hill town. (Tomio Ohashi).

中銀
中銀
Ginza DAI-ICHI HOTEL

A well-known visual illusion brings this out even more:
60 the famous 'duck-rabbit figure', which will be seen first one way then the other. Since we all have well learned visual codes for *both* animals, and even probably now a code for the hybrid monster with two heads, we can see it three ways. One view may predominate, according to either the strength of the code or according to the direction from which we see the figure at first. To get further readings ('bellows' or 'keyhole' etc.) is harder because these codes are less strong for this figure, they map less well than the primary ones – at least in our culture. The general point then is *that code restrictions based on learning and culture guide a reading, and that there are multiple codes, some of which may be in conflict across subcultures.* In very general terms there are two large subcultures: one with the modern code based on the training and ideology of modern architects, and another with the traditional code based on everyone's experience of normalised architectural elements. As I mentioned, (*above* page 24), there are very basic reasons why these codes may be at odds and architecture may be radically schizophrenic, both in its creation and interpretation. Since some buildings often incorporate various codes, they can be seen as mixed metaphors, and with opposing meanings: e.g. the 'harmonious, well-proportioned pure volume' of the modern architect becomes the 'shoe-box' or 'filing cabinet' to the public.

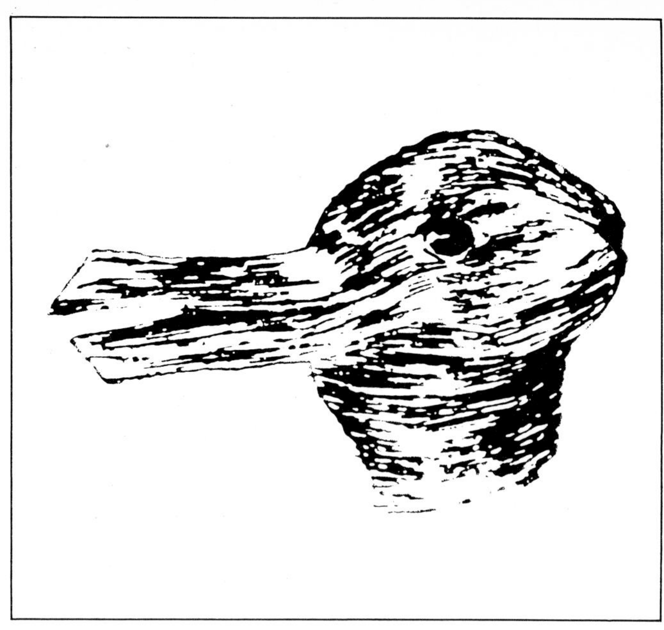

60 The DUCK-RABBIT ILLUSION, read from left to right by duck hunters and from right to left by frequenters of the Playboy Club. Since this illusion is so well known we can now see it as a new animal with two heads. But note: you can only read it one way at a time *depending on the code you choose to adopt.* (E. H. Gombrich, *Art and Illusion*).

61 JORN UTZON, *Sydney Opera House,* Australia, 1957–74. A mixed metaphor: the shells have symbolised flowers unfolding, sailboats in the harbour, fish swallowing each other and now, because of the local code, high cost. As with the Eiffel Tower, ambiguous meanings have finally transcended all possible functional considerations and the building has become simply a national symbol. This rare class of sign, like a Rorschach test, provokes response which focuses interest on the responder, not the sign. It could be called the 'enigmatic sign', because, like the ocean, it happily receives projected meanings from everyone. (New South Wales Government Office, London).

61 One modern building, the Sydney Opera House, has
provoked a superabundance of metaphorical responses,
both in the popular and professional press. The reasons
are, again, that the forms are both unfamiliar to architecture
and reminiscent of other visual objects. Most of the metaphors are organic: thus the architect, Jorn Utzon, showed
how the shells of the building related to the surface of a
sphere (like 'orange segments') and the wing of a bird in
flight. They also relate, obviously, to white sea shells, and
it is this metaphor, plus the comparison to the white sails
bobbing around in Sydney Harbour, that have become
journalistic clichés. This raises another obvious point with
unexpected implications: the interpretation of architectural metaphor is more elastic and dependent on *local*
codes than the interpretation of metaphor in spoken or
written language.

Some critics have pointed out that the superimposed
shells resemble the growth of a flower over time – the
unfolding of petals; while architectural students of Aus-
62 tralia caricatured this same aspect as 'turtles making love'.
From several points of view the violent aspect of broken
and smashed up shapes is apparent – 'a traffic accident
with no survivors'; while again these same views elicit
possible organic metaphors – 'fish swallowing each other'.
Reinforcing this interpretation are the shiny, scaly ele-
77 ments of the tiled surface which are apparent up close.
But the most extraordinary metaphor, and the one which

62 CARTOON presented by architectural students when Queen Elizabeth officially opened the building (from *Architecture in Australia*).

63 SYDNEY OPERA HOUSE, view of shells soaring and crashing, again an interesting ambiguity to be set along with the other mixed metaphors. Note the way the building glistens and takes on the cloud formations. (Australian Information Service).

Australians apply with a certain bemused affection, is 'scrum of nuns'. All those shells leaning over, confronting each other in two main directions, resemble the head-dresses and cowls of two opposed monastic orders, and the wildly unlikely idea that this could be a scrimmage of mother superiors dominates the possibilities. 'Wit' has been defined as 'the unlikely copulation of ideas together', and the more unlikely *but* successful the union, the more it will strike the viewer and stay in his mind. A witty building is one which permits us to make extraordinary but convincing associations.

The question obviously arises of how appropriate these metaphors are to the building's function and its symbolic role. Concentrating on this aspect and momentarily disregarding other things such as cost (the Australians spent something like twenty times the original estimate for their mixed metaphor) we might come to the following conclusion. On the one hand the organic metaphors are very appropriate to a cultural centre: images which suggest growth are particularly apt for meanings of creativity. The building flies, sails, splashes, curves up and unfolds like an animated vegetable. Fine. Perhaps if the building were renamed The Australian Cultural Centre (not the Sydney Opera House) and justified as a symbol of Australia's liberation from Anglo-Saxon dependence, (the overriding influence of Britain and America), then its interpretation might be clearer. We could then see these extraordinary metaphors in their most positive light, as symbols of Australia's break with colonial conformity and provinciality.

But doubts arise. We know the building was designed by a European (not an Australian) as an *opera* house – and one that works neither economically nor functionally in the manner it was conceived. Since such knowledge is an integral part of the code with which we interpret the building, our judgement cannot avoid being contaminated by this knowledge. It's rather like looking at the duck-rabbit figure: our perception is bent and shaped by codes based on previous experience. It is virtually impossible to perceive the building without knowing about the notorious 'Sydney Opera House Case', the firing of the architect, the cost, and so forth. So these local, specific meanings also become symbolised in the 'extravagant' shells.

Several modernists criticised the Opera House for other reasons: as a piece of literal communication the building tells you little and dissimulates much. You can't pick out the various theatres and restaurants and exhibition halls beneath the shells, which is why it has been so annoying to certain architects brought up in the tradition of expressive functionalism. They expect to see each function given a clear and separate volume, which ideally speaking, is an outline of the function – such as the 64
auditorium. They would have designed the building as a series of boxy fly towers and wedge shapes (the conventionalised 'word' for auditorium in modern architecture). The building violates this code, as classical architecture

64 KONSTANTIN MELNIKOV, *Russakov Club,* Moscow, 1928. The wedge shape plus rectangular flytower became established as the 'word' for auditorium in the language of modern architecture because of this building. The shapes follow, more or less, the volumes needed for the functions.

often did, by obscuring actual functions behind overall patterns. The debate then becomes whether such obscurantism is justified by the wit and appropriateness of the organic metaphor. I think it is, but others would deny this.

Perhaps one of them would be Robert Venturi, who also starts from the position that architecture should be looked at as communication, but comes to different conclusions from mine. He contends that buildings should look like
65 'decorated sheds, not ducks'. The decorated shed is a
66 simple enclosure with signs attached like a billboard, or the
application of conventional ornament, such as a pediment symbolising entry; whereas a duck, for him, is a building in the shape of its function, (a bird-shaped building selling duck decoys), or a modern building where the construction, structure and volume become the decoration. Clearly the Sydney Opera House is a duck for Venturi, and he wishes to underplay this form of expression because he thinks it has been overdone by the modern movement. I would disagree with this historical judgement, and take even greater exception to the attitudes implied behind it. Venturi, like the typical modernist that he wishes to supplant, is adopting the tactic of exclusive inversion. He is cutting out a whole area of architectural communication, duck buildings, (technically speaking **iconic** signs), in order to make his preferred mode, decorated sheds (**symbolic** signs) that much more potent. Thus we are being asked, once more by a modernist, in the name of rationality, to follow an exclusive, simplistic path. Clearly we need all the modes of communication at our disposal, not one or two; and it's the modernist commitment to architectural street-fighting that leads to such oversimplification, not a balanced theory of signification.

In any case, the Sydney Opera House does pose some difficult problems as a duck, because of its lack of a shared, public symbolism – a point Venturi's extreme position brings out. While the organic metaphors are suitable analogues for a culture centre, they are not reinforced by conventional signs which spring from the Australian vernacular, and therefore they have an erratic signification. Rather, they emanate from the widespread formalist movement of modern architects, a movement which might be more appropriately termed surrealist. Like a Magritte painting – the apple which expands to fill a whole room – the meaning is striking but enigmatic and ultimately evasive. What precisely is Utzon trying to say, beyond the primitive and exciting? Why, besides creativity, all the sails, shells, flowers, fish and nuns? Clearly our emotions are being heightened as an end in themselves, and there is no exact goal towards which all these meanings converge. They float around in our mind to pick up connections where they will, like a luxuriant dream following overindulgence.

They do however prove a general point about communication: the more the metaphors, the greater the drama, and the more they are slightly suggestive, the greater the mystery. A mixed metaphor is strong, as every student of Shakespeare knows, but a suggested one is powerful. In architecture, to name a metaphor is often to kill it, like analysing jokes. When hot dog stands are in the

65 ROBERT VENTURI, *The Duck versus Decorated Shed*. Venturi would prefer more decorated sheds, because he contends, they communicate effectively, and modern architects have for too long only designed 'ducks'. The duck is, in semiotic terms, an *iconic* sign, because the signifier (form) has certain aspects in common with the signified (content). The decorated shed depends on learned meanings – writing or decoration – which are *symbolic* signs.

66 SECURITY MARINE BANK, Wisconsin, c. 1971. The *symbolic* shed, one part communication of status and security, the other part function. Commercial pressures today naturally dissociate signifier and signified in this way, although not usually so clearly. (Wayne Attoe).

78 shape of hot dogs, then little work is left to the imagination, and all other metaphors are suppressed: they can't even suggest hamburgers. Yet even this kind of univalent metaphor, the Pop architecture of Los Angeles, has its imaginative and communicative side. For one thing, the customary scale and context are violently distorted, so the
67 ordinary object, for instance the doughnut, takes on a series of possible meanings not usually associated with this item of food. When it's blown up to thirty feet and built out of wood and sits on a small building, it becomes the Magritte object that has taken over the house from the occupants. Partly hostile and menacing, it is nevertheless a symbol of sugary breakfasts and *Gemütlichkeit*.

Secondly, an architecture made up from such signs communicates unambiguously to those moving fifty miles per hour through the city. In contrast with so much modern building, these iconic signs speak with exactitude and humour about their function. Their literalism, however infantile, articulates factual truths which Mies' work obscures, and there is a certain general pleasure (which doesn't escape children) in perceiving a sequence of them. Contrary to Venturi, we need more ducks; modern architects haven't propagated enough.

One who tried was Eero Saarinen. Immediately after he selected Utzon's Opera House as the winner of the competition, he returned to America and designed his own version of the curvilinear, shell building. The TWA ter-
69 minal in New York is an icon of a bird, and by extension, of aeroplane flight. In the details and merging of circulation lines, of passenger exits and crossways, it is a particularly clever working out of this metaphor. A
70 supporting strut is mapped to a bird's leg, the rain-spout becomes an ominous beak, an interior bridge covered in
71 blood-red carpet becomes, I suppose, the pulmonary artery. Here the imaginative meanings add up in an appropriate and calculated way, pointing towards a common metaphor of flight – the mutual interaction of these meanings produces a multivalent work of architecture.

67 HENRY J. GOODWIN, *Big Donut Drive-in*, Los Angeles, 1954. Originally there were ten of these giants, now there are, alas, three. The doughnuts sold are big.

68 DINOSAUR, Los Angeles, 1973. A curio shop which actually sells a few old bones, among other things. Los Angeles had a great deal of Pop architecture in the twenties and thirties, but most of it has been supplanted by the slick commercial symbols of chains, such as MacDonalds Hamburgers. (Environmental Communications).

69 EERO SAARINEN, *TWA Building,* New York, 1962. Designed after Saarinen judged the Sydney Opera House competition. Here the concrete shells are clearly recognisable as a metaphor of flight, although there are other animals suggested. (TWA).

70 TWA BUILDING. The leg of the bird is at the same time a beautiful abstraction of structural forces.

71 TWA BUILDING. The red carpet swoops over the entry space, curve and counter-curve reinforce the feeling of continuous movement – all appropriate for a transportation building.

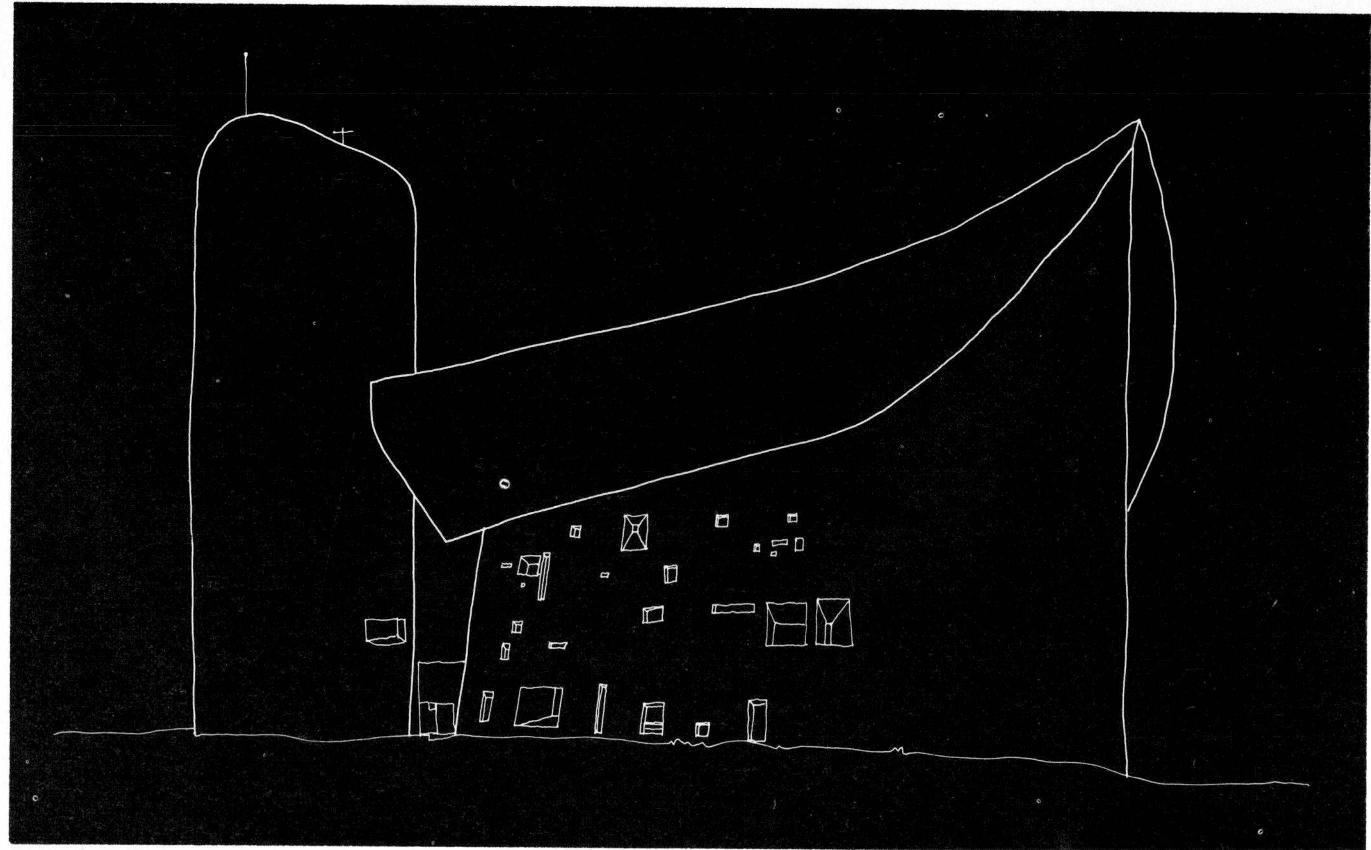

The most effective use of *suggested* metaphor that I can think of in modern architecture is Le Corbusier's chapel
72, 73 at Ronchamp which has been compared to all sorts of things, varying from the white houses of Mykonos to Swiss cheese. Part of its power is this suggestiveness – to mean many different things at once, to set the mind off on a wild goose chase where it actually catches the goose, among other animals. For instance a duck (once again this
90 famous character of modern architecture) is vaguely
89 suggested in the south elevation; but so also are a ship
88 and, appropriately, praying hands. The visual codes, which here take in both elitist and popular meanings, are working mostly on an unconscious level, unlike the hot dog stand. We read the metaphors immediately without bothering to name or draw them (as done here), and clearly the skill of the artist is dependent on his ability to call up our rich storehouse of visual images without our being aware of his intention. Perhaps it is also a somewhat unconscious process for him. Le Corbusier only admitted to two metaphors, both of which are esoteric: the 'visual acoustics' of the curving walls which shape the four horizons as if they were 'sounds', (responding in antiphony), and the 'crab shell' form of the roof. But the building has many more metaphors than this, so many that it is overcoded, saturated with possible interpretations. This explains why critics such as Pevsner and Stirling have found the building so upsetting, and others have found it so enigmatic. It seems to suggest precise ritualistic meanings, it looks like the temple of some very complicated sect which reached a high degree of metaphysical sophistication; whereas we *know* it is simply a pilgrimage chapel created by someone who believed in a natural religion, a pantheism.

Put another way, Ronchamp creates the fascination that the discovery of a new archaic language does; we stumble upon this Rosetta stone, this fragment of a lost civilisation, and every time we decode its surface we come up with coherent meanings we know do not refer to any precise social practice – as they appear to do. Le Corbusier has so overcoded his building with metaphor, and so precisely related part to part, that the meanings seem as if they had been fixed by countless generations engaged in ritual: something as rich as the delicate patterns of Islam, the exact iconology of Shinto, is suggested. How frustrating, how enjoyable it is to experience this game of signification, which we know rests mostly on imaginative brilliance.

72, 73 LE CORBUSIER, *Ronchamp Chapel,* France, 1955. View from the south-east. The building is over-coded with visual metaphors, and none of them is very explicit, so that the building seems always about to tell us something which we just can't place. The effect can be compared to having a word on the tip of your tongue which you can't quite remember. But the ambiguity can be dramatic, not frustrating – you search your memory for the possible clues.

74 RICARDO BOFILL and TALLER, *Walden Seven,* Barcelona, 1975. A gigantic hill of housing in red tile with twelve-storey holes cut into it, and punctuated by circular balconies. The layout of apartments is ingenious, but rather obvious living requirements have been sacrificed to achieve this image. Vertigo is a common reaction on the high bridges which overlook the communal space. The front door is a gestural joke.

75, 76 RICHARD ROGERS and RENZO PIANO, *Pompidou Centre,* Paris, 1976. (Richard Rogers).

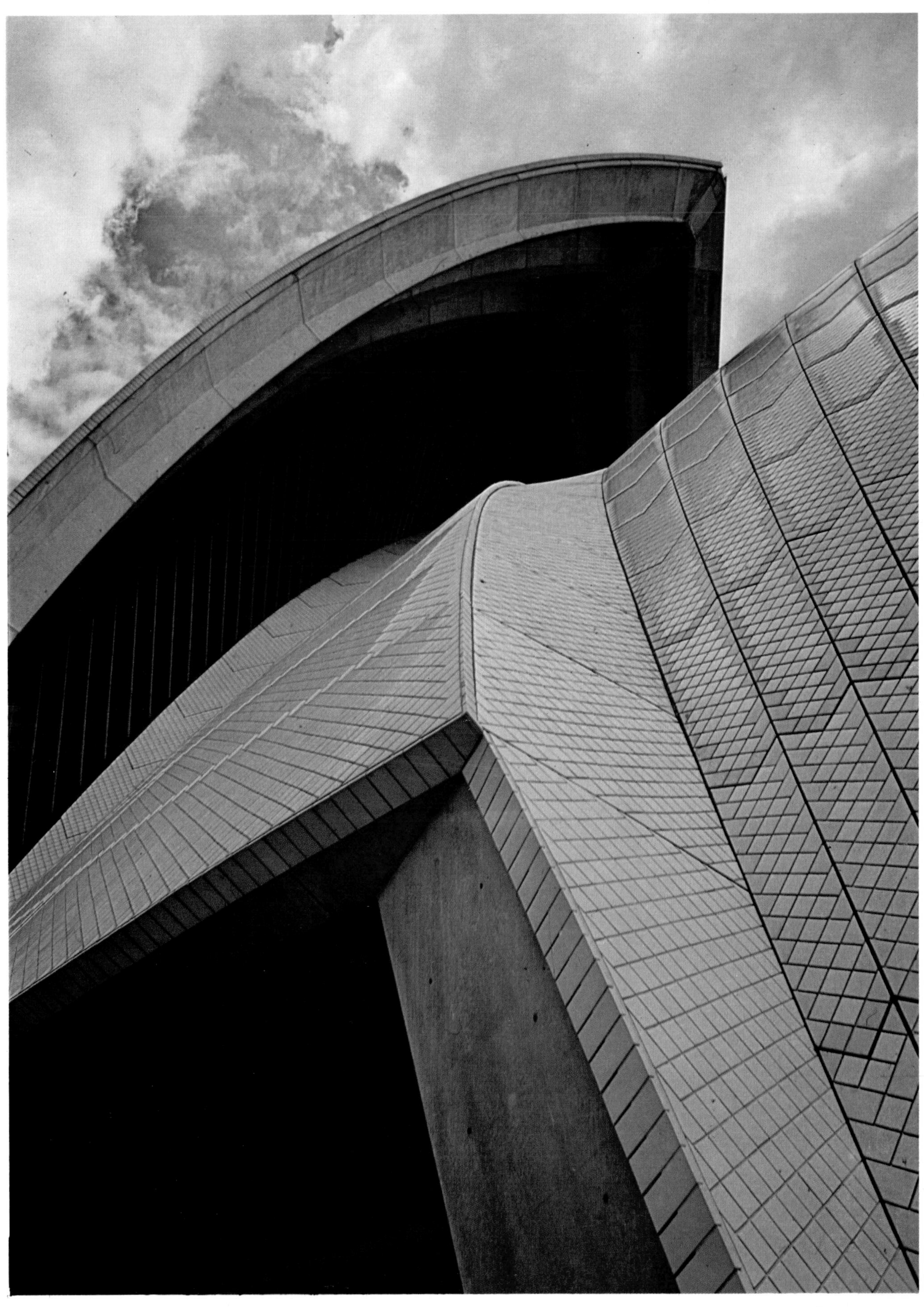

77 FISH SCALES and TURTLE SHELLS.

78 HOT DOG STAND, Los Angeles, c. 1938. Reinforced with additional signs such as oozing mustard, 'Tail-o-the-pup' etc. This architecture would appear to be unambiguous, yet at the Architectural Association in London, where I teach, it is classified in the slide library as a 'hamburger stand'. Once again, visual codes are mainly local.

79 BOOTMOBILE, Los Angeles, 1976.

80 MICHAEL GRAVES, *Benacerraf House addition,* Princeton, 1969. A Cubist syntax is used to call attention to itself. This heightening of our perception of doors, stairways, balustrades and views from a terrace is complex and masterful. It is so rich here that one forgets to ask what the functions are (actually an open terrace above, and a playroom and breakfast room below). Note how the structure, sometimes unnecessary, is pulled away from the wall. Railings and cut-out wall planes also serve to define a net of rectilinear space. The front balustrade is, conceptually, a column lying on its side – a play on syntactical meaning, as is the whole addition. (Laurin McCracken).

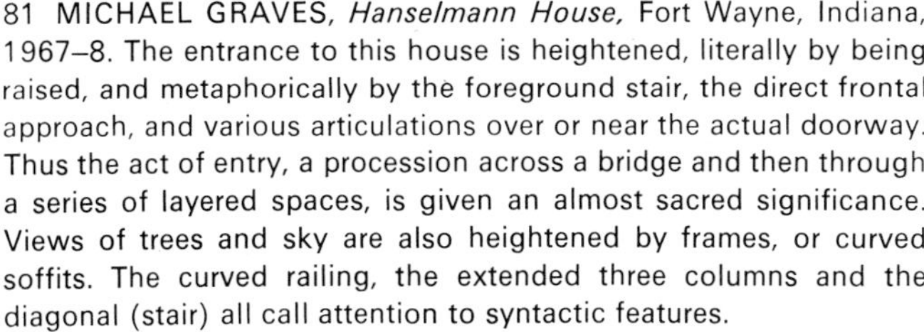

81 MICHAEL GRAVES, *Hanselmann House,* Fort Wayne, Indiana, 1967–8. The entrance to this house is heightened, literally by being raised, and metaphorically by the foreground stair, the direct frontal approach, and various articulations over or near the actual doorway. Thus the act of entry, a procession across a bridge and then through a series of layered spaces, is given an almost sacred significance. Views of trees and sky are also heightened by frames, or curved soffits. The curved railing, the extended three columns and the diagonal (stair) all call attention to syntactic features.

82 MICHAEL GRAVES, *Snyderman House,* Fort Wayne, Indiana, 1972. The intersection of two related syntaxes, Corbusier and Rationalist, set up actual semantic meanings: e.g. 'a war between a Mondrian and a Juan Gris', 'a stucco building trying to spring out of a prison cage', 'a collision of two ships', 'scaffolding' etc. This elaboration of a 1920s syntax is Baroque in every way but the curvilinear.

83 MINORU TAKEYAMA, *Ni-Ban-Kahn,* Tokyo, 1970. Blown-up graphic devices advertise this collection of 14 bars in the area of Shinjuku, Tokyo, where there are over 20,000 bars. Takeyama uses bulls eyes and the red/white industrial code to compete in an area where no other architect or city planner has worked so effectively. The glass wall becomes a gigantic beacon advertisement at night.

84 LUCIEN KROLL and ATELIER, *Medical Faculty building,* University of Louvain, near Brussels, 1969–74. (Lucien Kroll).

86 ANTONIO GAUDI, *Guell Colony Church,* near Barcelona, 1908–15. This entrance porch to the crypt shows the columns leaning and twisting against each other, while the muscles and tendons articulate this dynamic play of forces. Several of the columns resemble the leaning trees, since they are finished with a bark-like stone. The brick domes are hyperbolic parabolas – the whole structure was worked out in model form prior to building. Unfortunately only the crypt was finished.

87 'HOUSE OF BONES', was the metaphor seen by the press at first.

Below
85 ANTONIO GAUDI, *Guell Park, undulating bench,* Barcelona, 1907–12. This snake-like bench undulates around a terrace which overlooks the city. Bits of ceramic, glass and bottle are collaged together into a surprisingly comfortable seat. The reason is that Gaudí apparently asked one of his workmen to strip and then took form-fitting measurements from his sitting body.(Escuela Tecnica Superior de Arquitectura de Barcelona).

88–92 METAPHORS of *Ronchamp,* drawn by Hillel Schocken in a seminar on architectural semiotics at the Architectural Association. The mapping is amazingly literal when compared to the actual views.

93 CESAR PELLI, *Pacific Design Center,* Los Angeles, 1976. A long, high building which looks like an extruded moulding, among other things, because its section is projected throughout the building and on the end elevations. This metaphor is appropriate to its function, since the building displays the mouldings of interior designers (among other products). Its blue exterior, in translucent, transparent and reflective glass, gives it a startling presence in Los Angeles; and because of its size, it is known as 'The Blue Whale'. (Marvin Rand).

Opposite
94 PDC metaphors seen in a seminar on architectural semiotics, UCLA, 1976, drawn by Kamran. The metaphors were voted on by the class and placed in the following order of plausibility: **1** aircraft hangar, **2** extrusion or architectural moulding, **3** station or terminal building, **4** model of a building, **5** warehouse, **6** blue ice-berg, **7** prison, **8** a child's building-blocks or puzzle. The fact that so many metaphors turned out to be actual building types (e.g. 'station or terminal') shows that the PDC recalls other architecture quite strongly.

Another modern building which crystallises a series of metaphors, because of its unusual shape, is Cesar Pelli's
93 Pacific Design Center in Los Angeles – known locally as 'the Blue Whale'. Opposed to Ronchamp and TWA, it makes use of rectilinear forms and a curtain wall of three different types of glass, but these familiar elements nonetheless call up unfamiliar associations because of their peculiar treatment: 'iceberg', 'cash register', 'aircraft hangar', and most appropriately 'extruded architectural moulding', (it's a centre for interior decorators and
94 designers).

These metaphors can be mapped quite literally in terms of outline shape and section; not so the 'Blue Whale' image which relates only in terms of colour and mass. And yet this is the favoured nickname. Why? Because there happens to be a local restaurant whose doorway is a large blue whale's mouth, and the building is recognised as a leviathan in its small-scaled neighbourhood swallowing up all the little fish, (in this case the diminutive decorators shops). In other words, two local pertinent codes, the large scale and the connection with the local restaurant, take precedence over the more plausible metaphors of the building, the aircraft hangar or moulding – a good example of the way architecture is even more at the mercy of the perceiver than, say, poetry.

Architecture as a language is much more malleable than the spoken language, and subject to the transformations of short-lived codes. While a building may stand 300 years, the way people regard and use it may change every ten years. It would be perverse to rewrite Shakespearean sonnets, change love poetry to hate letters, read comedy as tragedy; but it is perfectly acceptable to hang washing on decorative balustrades, convert a church into a concert hall, and use a building every day while never looking at it, (actually the norm). Architecture is often experienced inattentively or with the greatest prejudice of mood and will – exactly opposite to the way one is supposed to experience a symphony or work of art.[12] One implication of this for architecture is that, among other things, the architect must overcode his buildings, using a redundancy of popular signs and metaphors, if his work is to communicate as intended and survive the transformation of fast-changing codes.

Surprisingly, many modern architects deny this most potent metaphorical level of meaning. They find it non-functional and personal, literary and vague, certainly not something they can consciously control and use appropriately. Instead they concentrate on the supposedly rational aspects of design – the cost and function, as they narrowly define them. The result is that their inadvertent metaphors take metaphorical revenge and kick them in the behind: their buildings end up looking like metaphors of

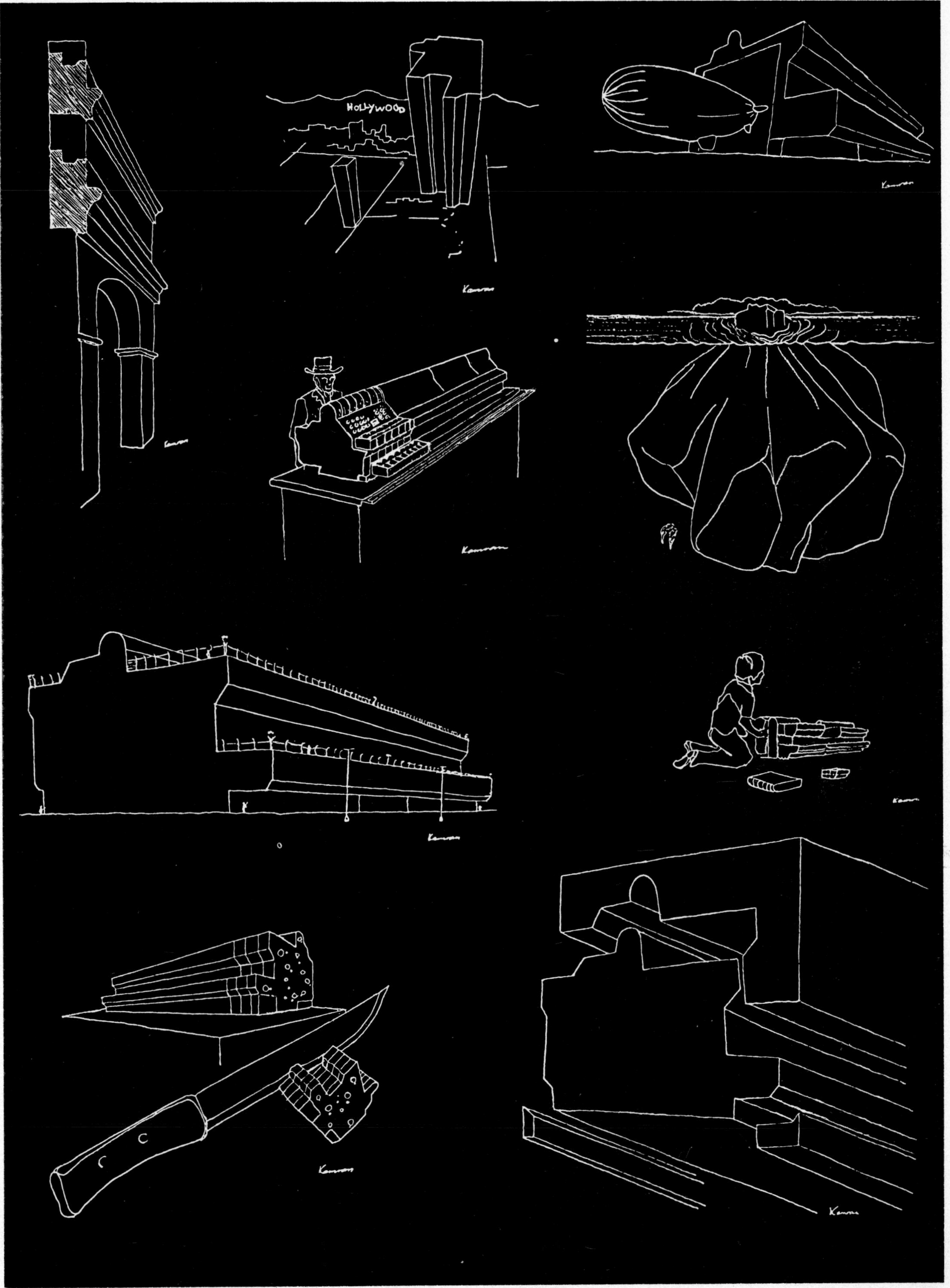
HOLLYWOOD

95 MANUFACTURERS HANOVER TRUST, New York, 1970. This kind of building on Park Avenue and elsewhere is often satirised by cartoonists such as Steinburg and Kovarsky, who will represent it as grid paper, bank account statement, or any number of economic graphs which rise and fall.

95 function and economics, and are condemned as such. The situation is bound to change, however, as both social research and architectural semiotics demonstrate the interpersonal, shared response to metaphor. This is much more predictable and controllable than architects have thought; and since metaphor plays a predominant role in the public's acceptance or rejection of buildings, one can bet that architects will see the point, if only for their own prosperity. Metaphor, seen through conventional visual codes, differs from group to group; but it can be coherently, if not precisely, delineated for all these groups in a society.

Words

Underlying much of what I have been saying so far is the notion of cliché – the fact that the architectural language, like the spoken one, must use known units of meaning. To make the linguistic analogy complete, we could call these units architectural 'words'. There are dictionaries of architecture which define the meanings of these words: doors, windows, columns, partitions, cantilevers, and so forth. Obviously these repeated elements are a necessity of architectural practice. The building industry standardises countless products, (there are over 400 building systems in Britain), and the architectural office repeats its favourite details.

As in language, yesterday's creative metaphor becomes today's tired usage, a conventional word. I have mentioned that the wedge shape became a sign of auditoria, and that concrete grills – the cheesegrater metaphor – became, largely, the sign of a parking garage ('office' is the secondary usage). Yet there is a crucial difference between the 'words' of architecture and of speech. Consider
the case of the column. A column on a building is one 96
thing, the Nelson Column in Trafalgar Square another, the 97
column smoke-stack at Battersea Power Station in 98
London a third, and Adolf Loos' entry for the Chicago 99
Tribune Column a fourth. If the column is a 'word', then
the word has become a phrase, a sentence and finally a 100
whole novel. Clearly architectural words are more elastic and polymorphous than those of spoken or written language, and are more based on their physical context and the code of the viewer for their specific sense. To determine what 'Nelson's Column' means you have to analyse the social-physical context, ('Trafalgar Square as a centre for political rallies'), the semantic overtones of Nelson, ('naval victories,' 'historical figure' etc.), the syntactic markers, ('standing alone', 'surrounded by open space and fountains'), and the historical connotations of column, ('use on temples', 'Three Orders', 'phallic symbol' etc.). Such an analysis is beyond the scope of this book, but an initial attempt has been made for analysing the column in general, which shows how fruitful this can be.[11] We can make a componential analysis of architectural elements and find out which are, for any culture, distinctive units.

Modern architects have not always faced up to the implications of clichés, or traditional words. They have, by and large, tried to avoid the re-use of **symbolic signs** (the technical term for meaning set by conventional usage)

96–100 The COLUMN as a 'WORD', seen in different contexts, changes its meaning. At ST MARTIN-IN-THE-FIELD, London, 1726, it is seen on a portico with other columns of the same order – clearly signifying 'colonnade', 'entrance', 'public building' as well as historical associations. The NELSON COLUMN, Trafalgar Square, 1860, shifts the semantic overtones towards commemoration, 'victory', 'politics'. 'standing alone' etc. The COLUMN-SMOKE-STACKS at BATTERSEA POWER STATION, London, 1929–55, have entirely different associations, because of their syntactic properties. They are placed above a massive base on four corners (incidentally this is now *the* sign of power station), and so the building looks mildly like an overturned table. Smoke belches out the top – which has no capital or entablature – so the 'fluted columns have been violated'. Adolf Loos' CHICAGO TRIBUNE COLUMN, a competition entry for a newspaper, was a double pun on the word column ('newspaper column', 'tribune', the name of the newspaper). Loos felt that the Doric Order was a most basic statement of architectural order and therefore fitting for a monument. Finally, the KENTON COUNTY WATER TOWER, Ohio, 1955, again shows the polyvalent aspect of this vertical shape, how it can be used on elevator shafts, chimneys, rocket launchers and oil derricks. Because of the column's positive associations with antiquity, it is often used as a disguise for such 'practical and prosaic' functions.

101, 102 LE CORBUSIER, *Pessac Housing,* before and after, 1925 and 1969. Ground floors were walled up, pitched roofs were added, the ribbon windows were divided up, terraces were turned into extra bedrooms, and a great number of signs which connoted 'security', 'home', 'ownership', were placed all over the exterior, thus effectively destroying the Purist language. (Architectural Association, Philippe Boudon).

because they felt these historical elements signified lack of creativity. For Frank Lloyd Wright and Walter Gropius the use of historical elements even signified lack of integrity and character. An architect who used the symbolic sign was probably insincere and certainly snobbish – the Classical Orders were a kind of pretentious Latin, not the everyday vernacular of industrial building and sober utility. From these latter building tasks a universal language, they hoped, could be constructed, a sort of Esperanto of cross-cultural usage based on functional types. These signs would be **indexical** (either directly indicating their use, like arrows, linear corridors), or else **iconic**, in which case the form would be a diagram of its function (a structurally-shaped bridge, or even Venturi's duck). Modern architectural words would be limited to these types of sign.

The only problem with this approach is, however, that most architectural words are symbolic signs; certainly those that are most potent and persuasive are the ones which are learned and conventional, not 'natural'. The **symbolic** sign dominates the **indexical** and **iconic**, and even these latter depend somewhat on knowledge and convention for their correct interpretation. There was thus a devastating theoretical mistake at the very base of the modern language. It couldn't work the way the architects hoped because no living language can: they are all based mostly on learned conventions, on **symbolic** signs, not ones which can be understood directly, without training.

A good example of architects' mistaken attitude towards the symbolic sign is their treatment of the pitched roof,
which conventionally signifies 'home' in Northern 101
countries. The modern architect disregarded this custom 102

for functional and aesthetic reasons, to create roof gardens, more space, rectilinear form (Walter Gropius gave six rational reasons for designing flat roofs). Not surprisingly these flat-top buildings were regarded as alien, as insecure, even unfinished and 'without a head'. The houses had been decapitated. Many of the inhabitants of Le Corbusier's Pessac felt his stark white cubical forms lacked a proper sense of shelter and protection, so they shortened the ribbon windows, added shutters and more window mullions; they articulated the blank white surfaces with window boxes, cornices and eaves; and some put on the old Bordeaux sign of protection, the pitched roof. In short, they *systematically misunderstood* his Purist language and systematically redesigned it to incorporate their conventional signs of home.

In spite of the many flat-roofed housing estates today, certain unreconstructed people still go on in their incorrigible way thinking that pitched roofs mean shelter and psychological protection. Many studies have shown this, and a major building society in England, recognising the fact, has taken as its symbol an archetypal couple walking arm in arm under a pitched-roof umbrella. Since this sign exists and since repeated usage will always create the **symbolic** sign, the modern architect might change his attitude towards these conventions. He might regard them as powerful meanings to be used normally in a straightforward way, if only to catch the attention of an audience he wants to convert.

If one wants to change a culture's taste and behaviour, or at least influence these aspects, as modern architects have expressed a desire to do, then one has to speak the common language of the culture first. If the language and message are changed at the same time, then both will be systematically misunderstood and reinterpreted to fit the conventional categories, the habitual patterns of life. This is precisely what has happened with modern housing estates. Pruitt-Igoe and Pessac are the two most celebrated examples. A more promising approach for the modern architect, or social interventionist, would be to study the *popular* house in all its variety and see how it signifies a different way of life for different taste cultures and ethnic groups.

Broadly speaking, these groups are classified in socio-economic terms by sociologists and market researchers, even though there is a lot of overlap and borrowing between groups, and there are other forces at work.[12] The class influence on taste is only one of several influences. It seems to me more exact to speak of semiotic groups than class-based taste cultures, because those groups which share preferences of **meaning** have a life and continuity of their own, which is only lightly coloured by socio-economic background. Basically, semiotic groups are in different universes of signification and have different views of the good life. I will mention three versions of the popular house which spring from these different groups.

1 The ideal of many working-class families is to buy a detached, small house, a bungalow roughly similar to others in an area they know. The values expressed in these houses are security, ownership, separation (a free-standing building), and a kind of conservative anonymity (represented by conforming more or less to the norm of the area). Levittown in America, and the Ideal Home
103, Exhibition in Britain, as well as most buildings in both
104 countries, cater to this semiotic group. It could be called conservative or conformist, sensible or petit-bourgeois,

103 'POPULAR BUNGALOW', Wales, 1975. Speculative builders have dominated this market since Levittown set the lower middle-class standard. Obvious signs are always incorporated which vary in their sources: Georgian bay window versus rustic stone chimney; plastic shingle versus cottage sign; display of car versus front garden; detached from the group, yet in the style of the neighbourhood. These minor contradictions display just the right blend of personality and conformity.

104 The ETON HOUSE, *Ideal Home Exhibition*, London, 1974. The facial metaphor is often present at the Ideal Home Exhibition, with two or three examples strictly symmetrical about the front door ('mouth'). Various signs of status are tacked on (such as the fibreglass, Adam detailing), but the snobbism is more apparent than real: it is not meant to convince the neighbours that you sent your son to Eton, but simply to distinguish the building from 'council housing'. This is perhaps the strongest social motivation, the distinction between 'us' and 'them' (those 'controlled' by the government). Hence the Ideal Home styles are relatively permissive, including Swiss Chalet and American Ranch House. In fact for 1976, the Ideal British Home was Colonial, an unforeseen consequence of 1776.

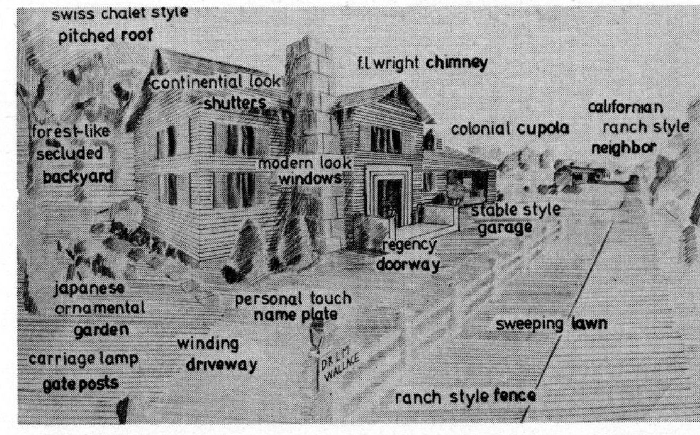

105 KEVIN FISHER, *English Popular House Analysis*, 1976. This synthesis of several reigning trends in the market shows how eclectic and permissive the popular English house is becoming. A pastiche of Japanese, American and English, modern and traditional, urban and rural. Few architects would dare use such a language because of its impurity, so the market remains open to the speculators. It is of course *possible* to use any language to send any message.

depending on which values are stressed and who is doing the valuing, because all these aspects are very clearly signified in the language. The archetype is a two-storey house with a central doorway, a symmetrical displacement of windows on either side, a chimney and pitched roof – all of which vaguely resembles a face with two eyes (top windows), nose (entrance portico) and mouth (doorway).

The band of planting in front of the house could be the shirt collar or moustache, symbolic 'moat', or 'forest', depending on what other signs are stressed. Since this group often wants to signal its new-found independence, meanings tend to support the old Anglo-Saxon maxim, 'every man's home is his castle' – and the castle may be defended by a picket fence or garden gnomes. There is a stately avenue winding to the front door – the curved pathway; past sylvan forests – bushes.

2 The next semiotic group tends to take the previous values for granted, since it hasn't just left what is regarded as the teeming city. In America this group might be called middle-class fastidious, since the clipped lawns and status signs of colonial provenance (nearly always false) harangue the passerby like some Bicentennial orator in a fit of nationalism. Indeed, cleanliness and caution, hard

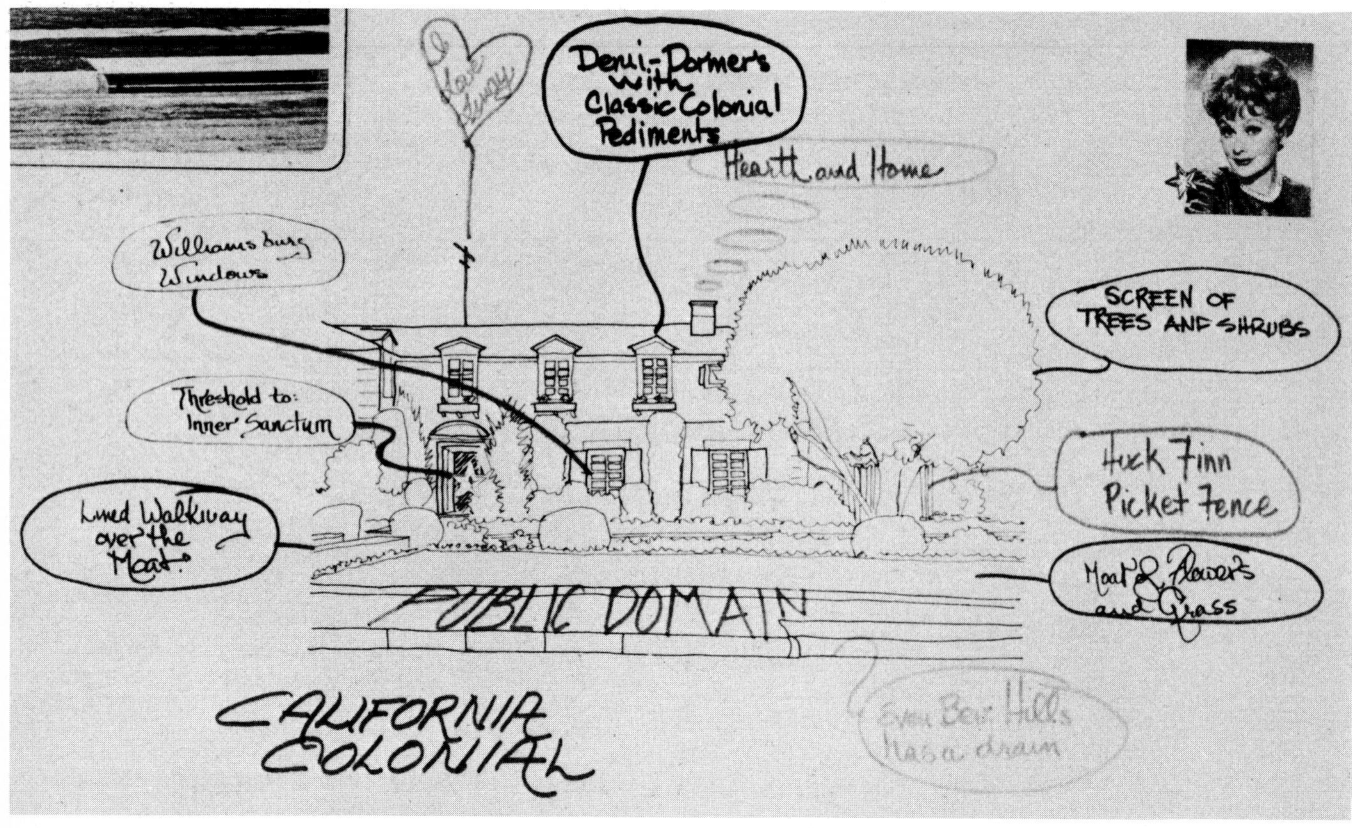

106, 107 LUCILLE BALL'S *House,* Beverly Hills, c. 1955. Movie Star House tourism has been a mass industry since the twenties, and maps are thankfully provided for visiting anthropologists. The habitat and layout of these houses is so conventionalised as to constitute a norm: first a public street and sidewalk, then a layer of manicured verdure discreetly signifying privacy, then the rambling house in one of five acceptable styles; the garage to one side. Behind this the tennis court, swimming pool and shrine room where the star's previous triumphs are shown to invited guests. This screening room often doubles as an exercise and game room, since physical fitness and relaxation are the two major drives of this tribe. The 'California Colonial' of Lucille Ball's house, with its raised eyebrow dormers, is the most popular style, followed closely by pseudo-Tudor. (Carol Barkin and Stephanie Vaughan).

work and discretion, prosperity and sobriety – all the images of WASP success – are there to brand this as the ultimate bourgeois dream. The only problem with this classification is that the appeal of these values reaches much further than the middle class.

For instance, the reigning style of movie star houses,
06- those of Beverly Hills and Bel Air which sell from a
09 quarter of a million dollars to three million, fall in this category. The movie stars clearly aren't middle-class, even if their tastes look it and they've come from this background. Are they slumming, or have they just adopted a previously existing semiotic tradition and then amplified it? Often they are called the 'aristocracy of America', because their values and way of life have become the standard of emulation for the mass of America. Films, and countless sightseeing bus trips going past the stars' houses, (a minor industry since 1922), have made these buildings the most influential in popular taste. They tend to be in one of six styles: **1** Southern Mansion, **2** Old English, **3** New England Colonial, **4** French Provincial/Regency, **5** Spanish Colonial, or **6** Contemporary/Colonial Hybrid. These are also the six reigning styles of the popular suburban house. A close investigation will reveal that most of these houses are Ersatz. That is, few of

108, 109 JIMMY STEWART'S *House*, Beverly Hills, c. 1940. A very fastidious mixture of Tudor and Japanese architecture with Swiss accents. The clarity of outline, the black and white alternations, the very studied informality of massing and planting send out a clear message. Such houses, often exposed in films, have confirmed if not created the American Dream House. Similar examples can be found outside every major city from Boston to Los Angeles, and since the norm is so invariable it almost constitutes a 'language without speech'. Put another way one could say that the language itself does the talking and the designer is a mouthpiece of this language. (Carol Barkin and Stephanie Vaughan).

them are serious, scholarly revivals, there is almost no pretence to historical accuracy or serious eclecticism. The styles are notional, **signs** of status and historical roots – but signs meant to remind you of the past, not convince you that the building is living in the present. There are
111, amusing cases when the signs become the whole building
112 itself.

3 Another semiotic group distinguishes itself from the previous one by inverting these signs and values. A studied casualness is preferred to fastidiousness, a kind of seedy, unselfconscious comfort is preferred to blatant order and rectitude. The down-at-the-heels aristocrat and the intellectual, the drop-out and left wing socialite all unite against what they take to be the vulgarity of the previous group's 'good taste'. Even the modern architect unites with them on this score.

Thus we find the emphasis on nature and **naturalness,** the building isolated and hidden in the actual woods, (as opposed to bushes), which are not manicured to near perfection. They are allowed to grow almost freely, just cut back at certain points to reveal a gable here, a roof there, as if by felicitous chance. In fact it is our old friend the picturesque tradition, the celebration of the carefully

110, 111 DISSEMINATION of the Movie Star Language, *Gay Eclectic House,* in the lesser side of Beverly Hills, conversion c. 1975. Analysis by Arloa Paquin. In this area interior decorators and others have started to convert their 1930 bungalows. Starting from a 20ft stucco box, they add on a false brick front (in this case), with carport, grillwork and 'false' shingles and Mexican beams. Some of these distortions of the code are amusing. Others are creative, most are cloying; but the language is at least being used (instead of entirely dominating the speaker).

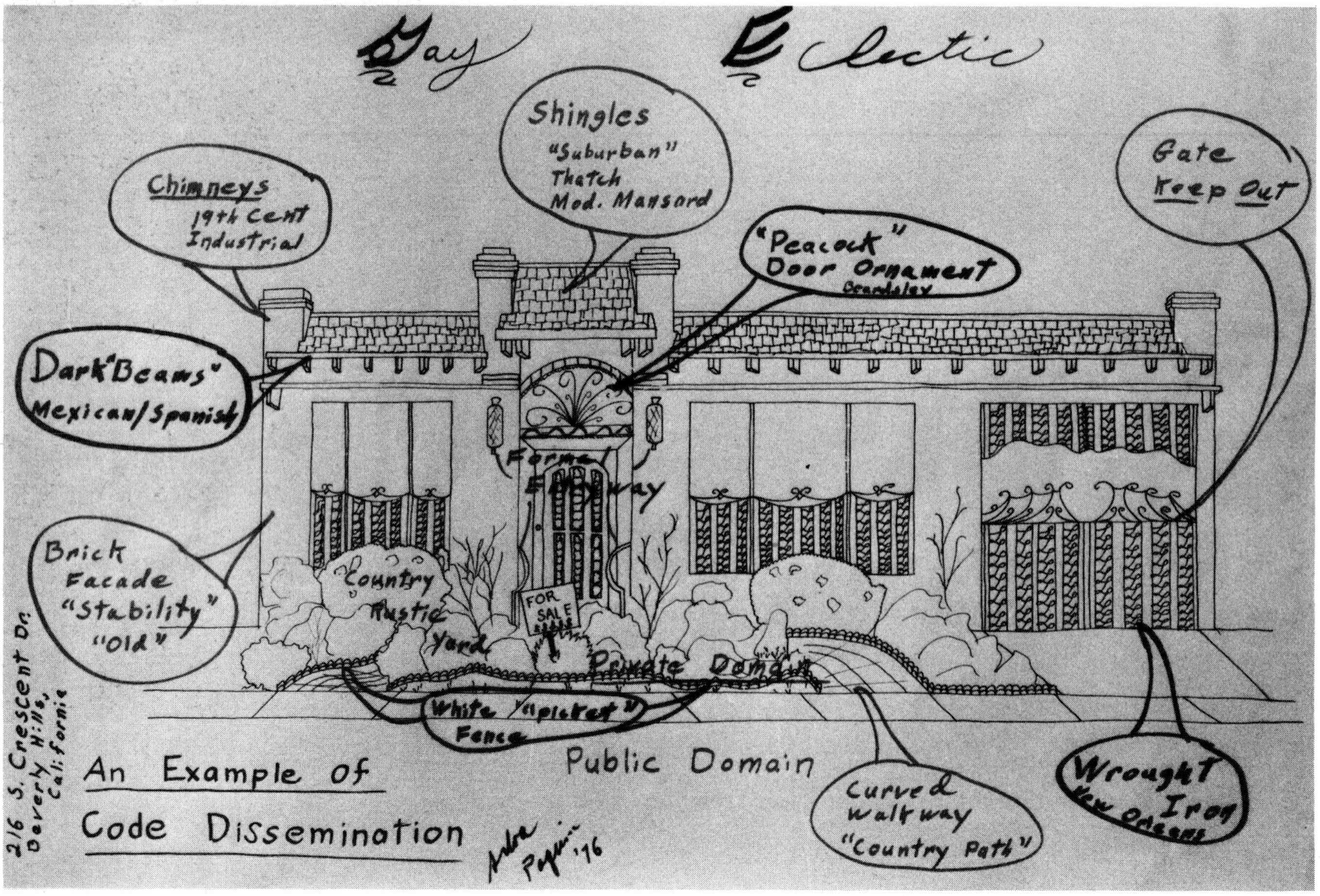

112 'HEDGE HOUSE', Beverly Hills, California, c. 1965. There is nothing much left of the old modern architecture which the owner disliked and covered with various 'natural' signs of planting. These clipped bushes, manicured to fit in the remaining fascia, heighten the act of entry and 'protect' the doorway. They have become conventional signs mandatory for all movie star houses.

careless and studied accident, in a variety of new clothes. These may be the white modern architecture of the 1920s, (*Le Style Corbu* has actually become a popular status-badge when handled by Richard Meier), the stick-and-shed style of the 1960s, or the House and Garden style of the last seventy years, represented on a collective level by such resorts and communities as Portmeirion and Port Grimaud.

114, Portmeirion is a misplaced Italian hill town set on the
115 lush Welsh coast, surrounded by two miles of rhododendron and other exotic overgrowth. Every vista is carefully composed as a landscape, each path wanders perfectly around every rock outcrop, each bush and flower relates miraculously to near and far buildings, and space ebbs and flows like water into small contained pools and dramatic, open cascades. *Trompe l'oeil*, phoney windows, buildings shrunken to five-sixths of their normal size, eye traps, calculated naivities, whimsical conceits (a sail boat is turned into concrete and thence into a retaining wall) – this sort of easy-going wit has proven popular with writers and tourists. The builder, Sir Clough William-Ellis, has cannibalised old buildings and preserved parts of them in his new confections.

114 SIR CLOUGH WILLIAM-ELLIS, *The Pantheon,* Portmeirion, 1926–66. A picturesque massing of foliage, and eclectic fragments cannibalised from destroyed monuments. Here an English lantern surmounts a Florentine dome painted day-glo green, which is on top of pink-Palladian walls, which is behind an actual Norman Shaw fireplace (through which you enter!).

115 PORTMEIRION, view into Battery Square, showing seaside architecture and Italian campanile. This stage-set architecture has, not surprisingly, been used in several films and commercials. This was the first creation of a formula that was later applied, in a cheapened version, to communities such as Port Grimaud, and ride-through parks such as Disneyland.

Opposite
113 RICHARD MEIER, *Douglas House,* Harbor Springs, Michigan, 1971–3. The villa in nature, enclosed, protected, and yet standing out as a man-made element. This Italian tradition, taken over equally by Le Corbusier and the upper classes, contrasts the raw and the cooked, the untouched and the finished. Here Meier uses a Corbusian syntax to represent the interior space, which is layered both horizontally and vertically through four storeys. (Ezra Stoller).

This care for the old and traditional is very apparent and one may take it as a characteristic sign of this semiotic group. The ancient is valued not so much for itself, but as a sign of continuity between generations and a connection with the past. While the first guess is that such values and understatements appeal only to elite tastes, this does not turn out to be true. For instance, 100,000 visitors come to Portmeirion every year, this sophisticated version of Disneyland; and millions visit country houses in England, mostly because of their rich historical associations.

These three semiotic groups, the conservative, the fastidious and the 'natural', hardly exhaust the plurality of taste cultures which exist in any large city. In America there is also the Main Street tradition, which Robert Venturi and Denise Scott Brown have analysed as a series of signs, and England has its counterpart in the High Street.

Venturi, Scott Brown and their team have been instrumental in calling attention to this wide area of symbolism,
116 and have put on an exhibition 'Signs and Symbols of American Life', which has presented some of the images that make up a popular language. Their own design, where possible, incorporates these signs, usually in an ironic
and esoteric way. While many critics deplore their work 117,
as unnecessarily banal, or ugly, or condescending – that is, 118
anything but popular – their deadpan approach is not necessarily a bad thing. After all, an architect may use a language without sending the customary messages, and if he wants to signify 'the ugly and ordinary' with this language he has a perfect right to do so. The Venturis justify their approach as social criticism: they want to express, in a gentle way, a mixed appreciation for the American Way of Life. Grudging respect, not total acceptance. They don't share all the values of a consumer society, but they want to speak to this society, even if partially in dissent. Also their sensibility is through and through modernist, their training has been in the language of Le Corbusier and Louis Kahn, so they cannot use popular signs in a relaxed and exuberant way – on a level with the Las Vegas sign artists whom they admire. But how could they? It takes years, perhaps a generation, to master the unselfconscious and conscious use of a new language, and so these architects are, to use a phrase borrowed from the Futurists, 'the primitives of a new sensibility'.

116 ROBERT VENTURI, DENISE SCOTT BROWN and TEAM, *The Street,* section from an exhibition 'Signs of Life: symbols in the American City', Renwick Gallery, Washington DC, 1976. Public buildings, state capitols, courts in a classicising style are mixed with the commercial vernacular. This exhibition documented popular symbolism in three major areas: the house, the main street, and the commercial strip. The 'lessons' that these designers drew favoured symbolic instead of sculptural architecture, 'decorated sheds' instead of 'ducks'. (Smithsonian Institution, Washington DC).

117, 118 VENTURI and RAUCH, *Tucker House,* Katonah, New York, 1975. The exterior exaggerates elements of the popular code – the overhanging eaves and picture window – while the interior uses the white, planar International Style as a backdrop for Kitsch and other objects. Actually, the fireplace with its round mirror is a miniature of the house, a very witty comment on the traditional idea of aedicules, miniature models and dolls houses. (Stephen Shore).

We may expect to see the next generation of architects using the new hybrid language with confidence. It will look more like Art Nouveau than the International Style, incorporating the rich frame of reference of the former, its wide metaphorical reach, its written signs and vulgarity, its symbolic signs and clichés – the full gamut of architectural expression.

Syntax

Another aspect architecture shares with language is more mundane than metaphors and words. A building has to stand up and be put together according to certain rules, or methods of joinery. The laws of gravity and geometry dictate such things as an up and down, a roof and floor and various storeys in between, just as the laws of sound and speech formation dictate certain vowels, consonants and ways of speaking them. These compelling forces create what could be called a syntax of architecture – that is the rules for combining the various words of door, window,
119 wall, and so forth. Most doors, for instance, follow the syntactical rule requiring a floor, necessarily flat, on both sides. What happens when this rule is constantly broken? The fun-house at the Amusement Park – which takes advantage of the fact that the nervous system unconsciously knows the syntactical rules and enjoys having them broken from time to time. Delirious word-salads, the speech of schizophrenics and poetry, all distort conventional grammar. It is obviously one of the defining characteristics of all sign systems used aesthetically. They call attention to the language itself by misuse, exaggeration, repetition, and all the devices of rhetorical skill.

Michael Graves speaks about 'foregrounding' the elements of architecture by turning them on their side, extending them out from their usual, functional context and painting them like a Juan Gris Cubist composition. His houses are poetic distortions of a Cubist syntax, whose only fault, in terms of communication, is in the choice of a limited syntax and undercoding. You need a reader's guide to appreciate the fact that a blue balustrade is a
column lying down. The Handmade Houses of the West 80
Coast use a much more accessible syntax in a similar way. 120
Shingles, wood siding, different types of standard windows tipped on their sides, placed at the corner of the building, roofs pitching at odd angles, logs used without finishing – these syntactical tricks have a richer resonance of meaning, except, of course, for those trained in synthetic cubism. Again it is a matter of coding and richness of coding which is at stake, not an absolute difference in meaning.

The syntax of architecture has preoccupied the modern movement to the point of obsession, which is one reason it will not be emphasised here. Starting with nineteenth-century theorists, Viollet-le-Duc, Semper and Choisy, this interest was soon idolised and became the dominant meaning of architecture. It's as if all that architecture suddenly had to talk about was its constructional process, the way it was put together. Louis Kahn

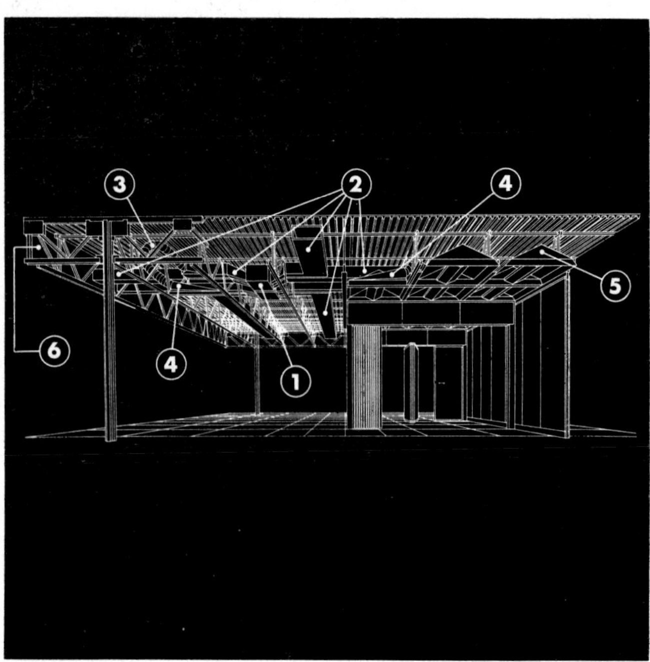

119 EZRA EHRENKRANTZ, *SCSD* (*Schools Construction System Development*), California, 1960s. The syntax of architecture obviously relates to functional concerns, as this drawing shows. Six major elements: **1** mixing boxes, **2** rigid ducts, **3** flexible ducts, **4** outlets, **5** lighting, **6** roof plenum, show the air-conditioning requirements. These were combined with roof, floor and a partition system to give a flexible syntax that could be changed in several ways. (Drawing by Mary Banham from *The Architecture of the Well-tempered Environment* by Reyner Banham.)

120 HANDMADE HOUSE, West Coast, c. 1970. Traditional wooden construction and ready-made windows and doors are displaced from their usual syntactic position to, again, call attention to themselves: 'The Window Building'. (From *Handmade Houses, A Guide to the Woodbutcher's Art,* by Art Boericke and Barry Shapiro, 1973. The owner and place are not identified).

wrote about THE FORM of building as if it were the Architectural Saviour which would rescue him from all other concerns.

Peter Eisenman produces beautiful syntactic knots which dazzle the eye, confuse the mind, and ultimately
21, signify *for him* the process that generated them. How
22 enticing; how banal. The spirit of process is supposed to lift you heavenwards so you overlook the prosaic assumptions. Once again, as with Mies, the analogy of beautifully consistent form is meant to stand for the missing values, transport the mind above ordinary concerns. But this Architectural Ascension is not quite miraculous enough; there is no lift-off, that is, syntactically speaking. Semantically, (a mode of communication Eisenman disdains), his buildings convey the sharp white light of rationality and the virtues of geometrical organisation: the exciting 'bridges to cross', surprising punched-out 'holes of space', the framed 'vistas', the Chinese puzzle of structure. So far as one can recognise these semantic meanings and connect them with other associations, (Protestantism, the white architecture of the twenties), then these buildings have a wider meaning. In other words, the pure realm of syntax is only relevant perceptually when it is incorporated into semantic fields.

Semantics

In the nineteenth century, when different styles of architecture were being revived, there was a fairly coherent doctrine of semantics which explained which style to use

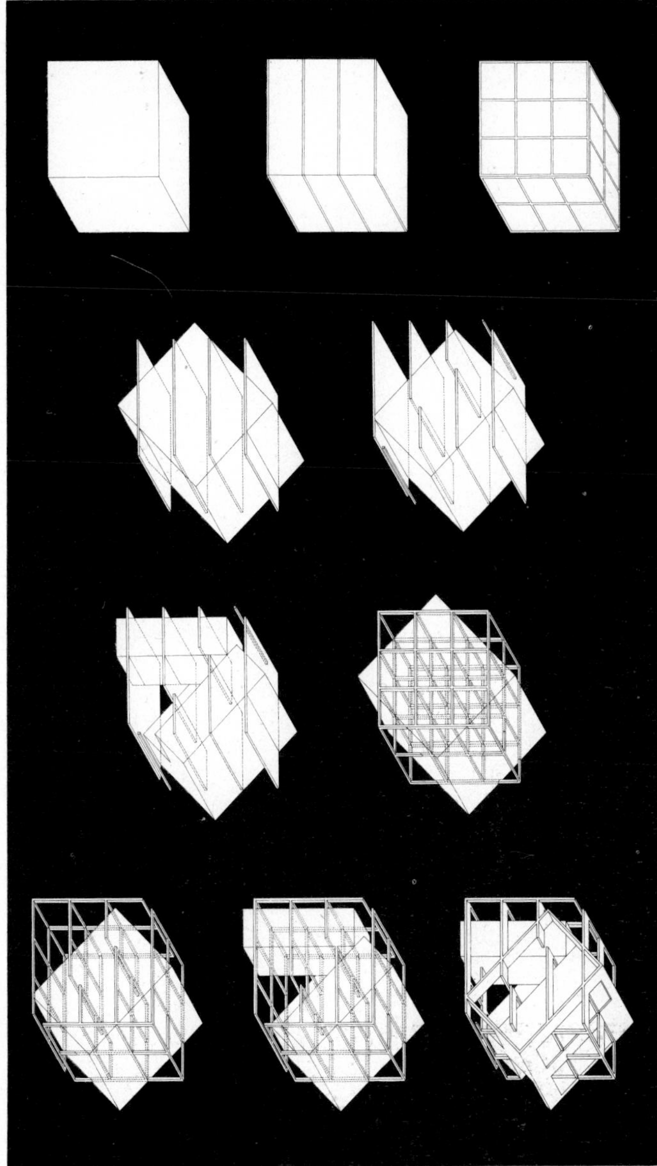

121, 122 PETER EISENMAN, *House III* for Robert Miller, Lakeville, Connecticut, 1971. Several of the drawings which generated the house show the main oppositions between two grids at 45° (step 6), a conceptual cage of boxed space (step 7), a column grid (step 3), and wall planes in 'shear' (step 5). Bridges and open volumes unite and divide the room functions. The facades 'mark' some interior transformations, that is if you look at them with the diagrams in your hand and think for a long time. This architecture, like nineteenth-century programme music, demands a complementary text in order to be fully understood.

123 J. C. LOUDON, *How to Dress a Utilitarian Cottage,* sketches from Loudon's *Encyclopaedia*. A basic cube with hipped roof is transformed with verandah and terrace, with trellis, with a castellated Gothic jacket, monastic habit and Elizabethan front. The suitability of style depends on the owner's role and place of residence.

124 THOMAS USTICK WALTER, *Moyamensing Prison,* Philadelphia, 1835. The Egyptian style, with its battered walls, heavy columns and small openings, naturally signified a structure from which it was hard to escape. (HABS, Library of Congress, photo Jack E. Boucher).

on which building type. An architect would pick the Doric Order for use on a bank because the Order and the banking function had certain overtones in common: sobriety, impersonality, masculinity and rationality (a bank was meant to look tough enough to discourage robbers, and sensible enough to encourage depositors). Not only were these semantic properties set by comparison, by looking at the Orders in opposition to each other and other styles, but so were a host of syntactic aspects: the size of the Doric capital, the column's relation to other columns, and its proportion to the cornice, frieze and base. Since these forms and relationships were used coherently, people felt able to pass judgement on their *suitability*. They could tell what the building signified, and they could read a slight change in emphasis, a variation of proportion, as a change in meaning.

Of course, this is to idealise the situation, as only a small part of the community could make these distinctions. But at least *some* could, and this community (echoing the root-word 'communication') kept the architect responsive to the whole enjoyable game of signification. He knew that if the semantic system were violently overthrown or became too complicated, his communication would be reduced to primitive gestures. In fact, by 1860 the game of eclecticism had become too complicated. For this reason it was overthrown, and vilified sixty years later because it had failed to signify those meanings architects found important. But it needn't have broken down if an adequate theory of eclecticism had been in operation. (I can't discover anything of that time that develops much beyond the notion of syncretism: taking the best parts from different buildings and combining them).

Nonetheless, revivalist architects did at least justify their choice of a style in terms of appropriateness, suitability; and this gave a degree of coherence to their formal choice. One architect, J. C. Loudon, proposed a theory of 'associationism' based on the notion of 'association of ideas', and even went so far as to say that each house should convey in its manner the character and role of its owner.[13] If the inhabitant were a country parson, the
house should be dressed in castellated Gothic or related 123
clothing. Thus the environment would become more and more legible as society became more differentiated.

To a certain extent this doctrine was followed in the nineteenth century, and you find that the introduction of a new style is assimilated into the appropriate semantic field. The Neo-Egyptian Style, popular in 1830 because of the Rosetta Stone and Napoleon's previous campaigns, was used sensibly on banks, tombs, prisons and medical colleges. The argument for its use might be based either on **conventional** or **natural** meanings. In the first cases, Neo-Egyptian was appropriate because the Pharaohs buried their treasure in temples of this style; or famous Egyptian doctors, healers and practitioners of medicine were sometimes also architects. Hence by the association of ideas, you could properly use the Egyptian style on banks and chemists' shops. Secondly, this style had natural meanings of heaviness, impenetrability and massiveness. The walls are battered and the openings small – use it on prisons, it 'naturally' signifies high security.[14]

125 CHARLES GARNIER, *Paris Opera House,* 1861–74. The giant, heroic order is played double height against a smaller one. Surfaces are covered with sculpture and polychromy. Everywhere statues take up operatic poses, flexing their muscles – even the women look intimidating. The interior grand staircase displays people as if they were to make an entrance on stage. The internal corner, with its re-entrant angles, medallions and general grandiloquence, is the most muscle-bound corner of the time. The Second Empire style *naturally* signified power: it took a lot of money to build. (French Government Tourist Office).

By the same line of reasoning, the Neo-Baroque, or Second Empire Style of 1860 had a series of natural overtones. It was massive, overarticulated, splendiferous, muscular, angst-ridden, tempestuous, bombastic, playful, exuberant, pretentious, and very expensive to build. Where should it be used? On the opera house of course.
125 Garnier's Parisian confection of the 1870s was most suitably clothed; and it was no accident that when he conquered France, Hitler danced a jig on its steps. His
126 choice of this style for the Third Reich (an Empire meant to last longer than the French attempts) was both appropriate and inadvertent. It symbolised strength, but like so many governments which have chosen this style, it was a strength that didn't survive its leader. Today, for this historical reason, it conventionally symbolises 'vanished power' or 'ineffectual dictatorship', and is used in innumerable movies and television dramas to signify this ambivalent pathos. The short-lived nature of the architectural code, and its distortion by historical events thus brings out once again the domination of conventional meaning over natural signification.

We can clarify this issue by looking at the classical language of architecture, the way the Three Orders constituted a semantic system, and how this system changed under the pressures of eclecticism. Vitruvius characterised the Doric Order as bold, severe, simple, blunt, true, honest, straightforward, and in sexual terms, masculine. In part this characterisation stemmed from the natural metaphors inherent in this form, but also it stemmed from historical accident (or at least Vitruvius' account of the Doric Order's birth).

The Corinthian Order was, by contrast, delicate, dainty, slender, ornamental and, sexually speaking, a young virgin. As one would guess, the middle Order, the Ionic, was a kind of architectural hermaphrodite, a neuter – in fact for Vitruvius, a matronly Order, because it was slightly more feminine than masculine (with volutes that look elegant). But these characterisations really only begin to make sense, as E. H. Gombrich has pointed out, when the Orders are put *in opposition to each other*.

> The rigid orders of ancient architecture would seem to be a fairly recalcitrant matrix for the expression of psychological and physiognomic categories; still it makes sense when Vitruvius recommends Doric temples for Minerva, Mars, and Hercules, Corinthian ones for Venus, Flora, and Prosperina, while Juno, Diana, and other divinities who stand in between the two extremes, are given Ionic temples. Within the medium at the architects' disposal, Doric is clearly more virile than Corinthian. We say that Doric expresses the god's severity; it does, but only because it is on the more severe end of the scale and not because there is necessarily much in common between the god of war and the Doric order. (E. H. Gombrich, *Art and Illusion*, London, 1960, pp. 316–317.)

Clearly there is nothing in common between warfare and the Doric except with respect to comparable things or elements: they each occupy equivalent semantic zones. In other words, if we map the Three Orders in a
128 semantic space, it is the relationships (r1, r2, r3) which really matter, and not the 'natural' meanings of the forms, nor the particular semantic axes we choose, (whether Vitruvius' or our own).

As long as we can distinguish clear differences between elements, it doesn't matter too much what these differences are, because custom and usage will first set them in one semantic space and then transform them to another. This can be seen in the nineteenth century with the rapid shift of stylistic meanings. For instance, in very crude terms, the concept of state power was indicated successively by the Roman revival, the Greek neo-Classical, the Gothic (at least in the House of Parliament), the Italian High Renaissance, the *Rundbogenstil*, the High Victorian Gothic, and finally in the 1870s, the Second Empire Style. There was a general trend in this evolution towards more and more bombast and articulation, understood metaphors of power; but all of a sudden the semantic system could be overturned. Simplicity could become a correlate of potency, as it was with the Neo-Classical and the International Style. There is nothing to keep an age from inverting the semantic space of its predecessors. The relation of form to meaning is mostly conventional.

126 CHARLES GARNIER, *Paris Opera House*, 1861–74.

We can see this transformation of meanings in the jump from the Classical Language of architecture to Eclecticism, and in the work of one man. Nikolaus Pevsner has summarised the way John Nash used a different 'style for the job'.

> [Nash] had a nice sense of associational propriety;
> as shown in his choice of the neo-Classical for his 127

127 JOHN NASH, *Chester Terrace,* Regents Park, London, 1825. The Corinthian Order, triumphal arches, and endlessly repeated white forms were used on these town houses giving them an appropriate impersonality and rectitude. The detailing was notional and symbolic, quickly conceived for spec builders. For this kind of opportunism Nash was damned by the serious classicists. C. R. Cockerell: 'Greek bedevilled . . . scenographic tricks hastily thought, hastily executed . . .' The indictment may have its point, but still Nash's willingness to change to the appropriate semantic system has its greater point.

town house and of the Gothic for his country mansion (complete with Gothic conservatory). Moreover, he built Cronkhill in Shropshire (1802), as an Italianate villa with a round-arched loggia on slender columns and with the widely projecting eaves of the Southern farmhouse (Roscoe's *Lorenzo Medici* had come out in 1796); he built Blaise Castle, near Bristol (1809) in a rustic Old-English cottage style with barge-boarded gables and thatched roofs (one is reminded of the *Vicar of Wakefield*, Marie Antoinette's diary in the Park of Versailles, and Gainsborough's and Greuze's sweet peasant children),
130 and he continued the Brighton Pavilion in a 'Hindu' fashion, just introduced after 1800 at Sezincote in the Cotswolds where the owner, because of personal reminiscences, insisted on the style. 'Indian Gothic' . . . (Nikolaus Pevsner, *An Outline of European Architecture*, Harmondsworth, 1964, p. 378.)

In effect, Nash has substituted a revival style for each of
129 the Three Orders. Roughly speaking, Hindu has been substituted for Corinthian, Gothic for Ionic and Classical for Doric (the Old English and Italian styles occupy new niches).

More significantly, a single form has taken on its opposite meaning in the system. The Corinthian (or Nash's Classical Order) has become masculine, simple and straightforward, because now it is set against other formal elements. This inversion is a good illustration of the semiotic rule that it is relationships between elements which count more than their inherent meanings. We could find countless other examples throughout architectural history: the Picturesque aesthetic being 'functional' in 1840 and 'anti-functional' in 1920; simple, Platonic forms symbolising truth and honesty in 1540 and deceit and artifice in 1870, and so on. Although our intuition and perception of form may feel straightforward and 'natural', it is based on an elaborate set of changing conventions. It is the differences between juxtaposed elements which constitute one of the bases for their meaning – not the natural overtones inherent in the elements themselves.

Even though aesthetic and technical issues dominate architects today, they still pay some measure of attention to semantics. An architect will use a curtain wall for an office building, because glass and steel feel cold, impersonal, precise and ordered – the overtones of methodical business, rational planning and commercial transactions. 131

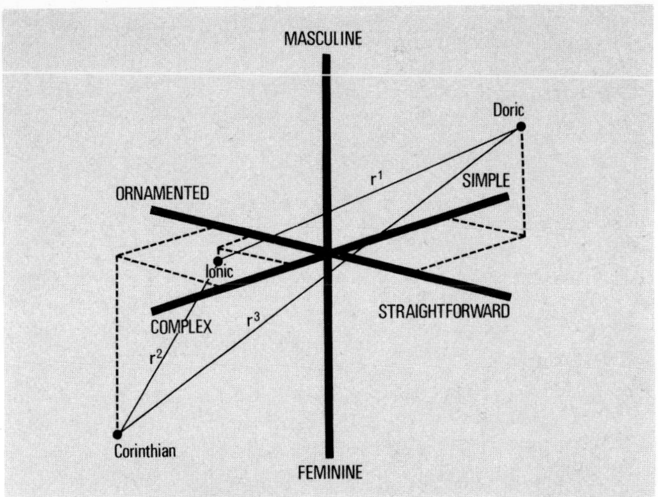

128 The THREE ORDERS. I have used these particular axes of Vitruvius for the sake of simplicity and comparison with the subsequent diagrams. But more interesting oppositions could be chosen as long as they are semantically distinct enough to give different information from each other. For instance, 'nature' might be opposed to 'culture', 'power' to 'impotence', etc. Semantic meaning consists partly in *oppositions within a system*.

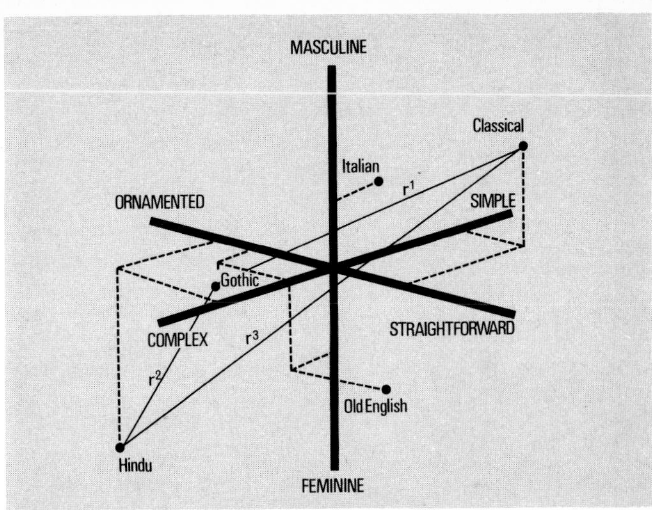

129 JOHN NASH'S *Five Styles* compared in the same semantic space as the Three Orders (128). The comparison brings out the fact that it is the *relationship* between styles, or Orders, which matters most in determining semantic meaning. The Corinthian, or Classical Order, has thus taken on its exact opposite meaning in Nash's system, because now it is more masculine, simple and straightforward than the Hindu style.

130 JOHN NASH, *Royal Pavilion*, Brighton, 1815–18. Nash threw into his soufflé a bit of Gothic, a bit of Chinese, a bit of cast-iron (palmtree columns), and his own version of a bulbous Hindu style. The domes are faintly mammarian. Here is the beginning of modern Ersatz, the first exuberant Kitsch building in England. Bad taste has been a positive creative force since then reaching one high with the Victorian country house. All this obscures, however, the appropriateness of choosing the Indian style for an escape palace next to the sea. If you are designing a 'pleasure dome' for the Prince who wants to get away from London sobriety, what better than the style of Kubla Khan (published 1816)?

131 NORMAN FOSTER, *Willis Faber Office,* Ipswich, 1975. Dark tinted solar glass and steel studs make this 'Big Black Piano' or 'Rolls-Royce' semantically fitting for cool office work. The building curves around the site, takes up the street lines and reflects the surrounding environment in fragments. (John Donat).

132 TRADITIONAL SWISS CHALET *'Montbovon'*, sixteenth-century, now in Geneva. The natural qualities of wood make it semantically suitable for the house. The knots, grain and texture are all metaphors for the wrinkles and birth marks on skin; the surface is tactile, warm and faintly responsive, again like the human body: the material can be easily tooled at a human scale. In this case the surface is adorned with jewellery and decorated like a peasant costume.

One could argue that the architect should deflect these meanings, that business might be made to look more adventurous and domestic than it is; yet the basic classification is suitable.

Wood is intrinsically warm, pliable, soft, organic, and
full of natural marks such as knots and grain, so it is used
domestically or where people come into close contact 132
with the building. Brick is associated by use with housing, and is inherently flexible in detail, so it is also used domestically. In spite of the fact that there are much more economic building systems available, the wood-and-brick hybrid still accounts for seventy-five per cent of speculative and council housing in Britain – a clear indication that semantic issues take precedence, in the public's mind, over technical ones.

What about new materials such as nylon, which make up pneumatic buildings? The inflatable system is naturally pudgy, squashy, cuddly, sexual, volumetric and pleasant to touch, so it has naturally found a secure niche in the semantic field and is used appropriately on swimming
pools, blow-up furniture, entertainment areas and other 133-
unmentionable places. Its occasional use as a church or 135
office building brings out different, less dominant semantic overtones.

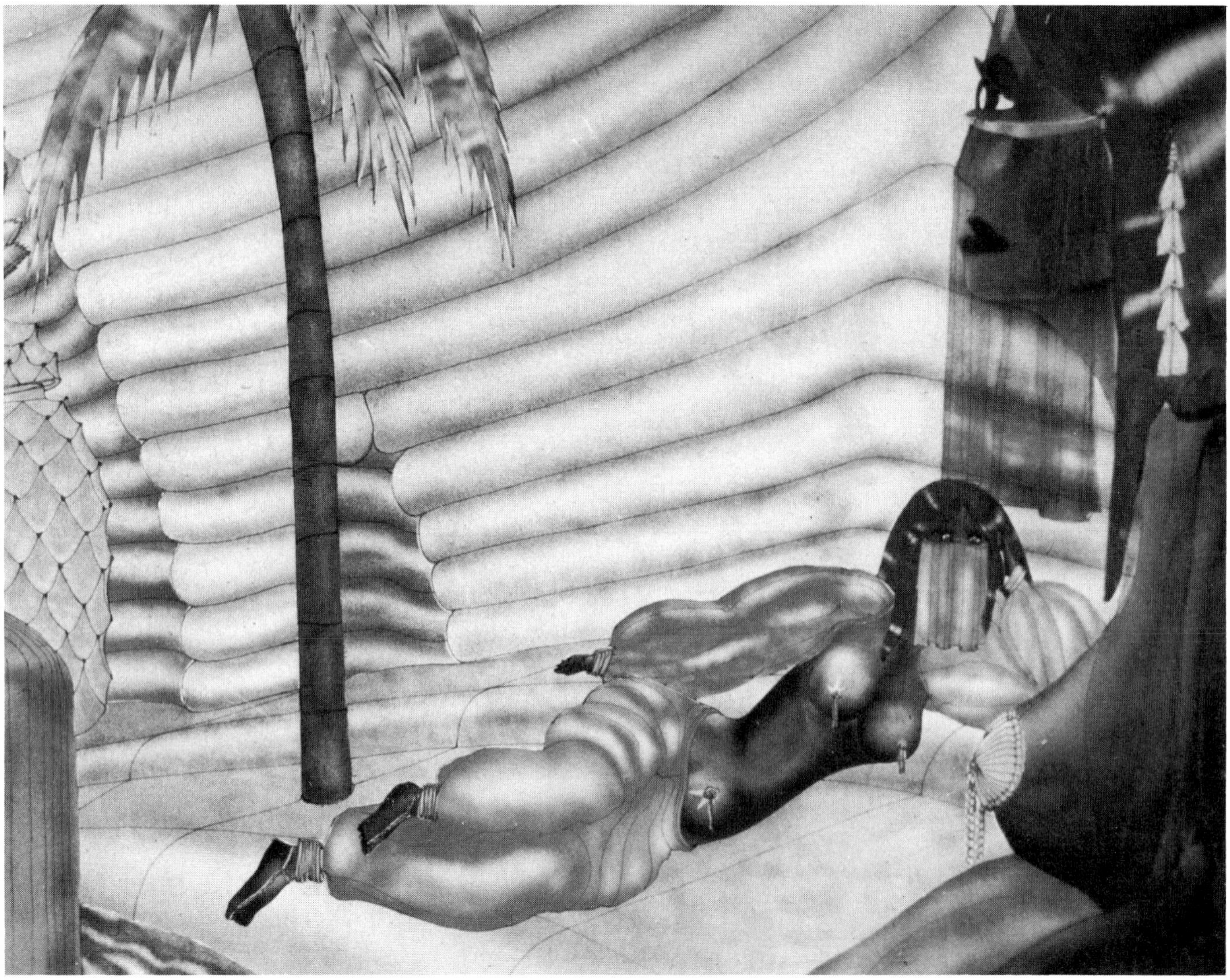

133 PAUL BURROWS, *Brothel for Oil Men in the Desert,* 1973. The pneumatic architecture takes up and supports the natural metaphors of these girls, as well as their activity.

134 BARBARELLA, 1968, is always shown surrounded with viscous, shiny plastic and soft, hairy fur. (ALA Fotocine).

135 JAMES BOND and TIFFANY CASE in *Diamonds Are Forever,* 1971, frolic around on a transparent water bed surrounded by 3,000 tropical fish. Connery's sardonic smile suggests he has had almost enough of this sort of thing. (United Artists).

These comparative aspects of building systems can be graphed in a semantic space similar to that already used, although axes other than the ones I have taken over from
136 Vitruvius would be more relevant. The **relations** between brick, pneumatics, concrete and steel set up the semantic field which will differ slightly for each individual and particular usage employed. Architects do not at present consciously map materials to each other, and functions to each other, and then compare the two mappings. Rather
137 they leave semantic questions to intuition, if they acknowledge them at all. Yet if our complex urban environments are to speak coherently, an explicit method must be used. The various building systems, the new materials, the five or so reigning styles, create such semantic richness as to generate confusion. So far architects have only responded to this as a positive aesthetic gain, trading off stylistic options for psychological and social meaning. As a result no one expects to understand a building and read it as a text. Everyone is the loser, the architect and public. Hence the plea that some system of semantic ordering be explicitly used. It can be as crude as the one proposed here, because it is gross distinctions and oppositions that are at stake, not the fine shades of semantic meaning (which can in any case only be communicated in language).

Several architects have made hesitant steps in this direction – hesitant because they are not backed up by theoretical understanding, or by more than single instances in their large output. One such building in Rome com-
138 pleted in 1965 has been rather heavily criticised for being made up of clichés, and for being schizophrenic. This building, by the Passarelli brothers, uses the conventional forms for office: smooth black steel and glass, below conventional signs for dwelling – hanging vines, broken silhouette, picturesque massing and balconies. A third building system below ground, in monolithic, Brutalist concrete, is the parking garage. The standard joke was that each of the brothers designed a different part of the building and never talked to each other. Part of the criticism directed against this building was for its obvious, boring use of styles already better developed by Harrison and Abromovitz, Paul Rudolph, and Le Corbusier; and one can see the point of this censure.

But also, and perhaps a more deep-rooted reason for the pique was the use of various structures and materials. Architects and critics brought up with the International Style were ingrained with the Purist notion that one aesthetic and structural system should be used on a building. Attendant ideas supporting this were the notions of harmony, the classical ideal that a part cannot be added or subtracted without disturbing the integrated whole, and that each building had, Platonically speaking, one and only one best solution.

There were even further assumptions which this building called into question: the self-conscious use of opposite styles *as styles*. Le Corbusier had said, 'the "styles" are a lie'. Frank Lloyd Wright and Walter Gropius believed that a single style, expressing the character and integrity of the architect, must animate all his work – otherwise he was guilty of insincerity, pandering to the whims of a client and ultimately to a corrupt ruling taste. Eclecticism meant slick facility and lack of conviction.

There are two obvious problems with this single-style approach (still the reigning one, even if it is less explicit than at previous times). First, mixed styles are an aid to communication, as the Passarelli building shows; and an architect must master at least three or four to articulate any complex building today, especially if he is to design the interior.

Secondly, the connection of any particular style with sincerity, whether it is the International Style or the *ad hoc* aesthetic of Handmade Houses, is a matter of history and convention, not something eternally true. By that typical process of historical inversion, we have actually arrived at a position where consistency and Purism do not equate with integrity, but quite the reverse. How has this happened?

Precisely because the International Style has been accepted on a massive scale by those who build cities. It is now the conventional style of the ruling class and its bureaucracy, (at least for its large-scale offices and civic

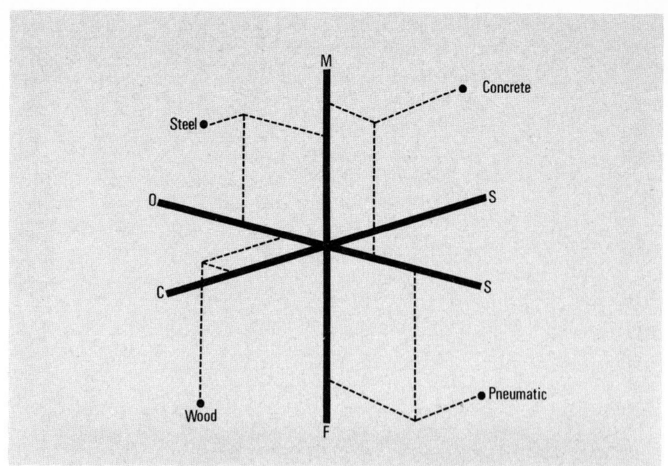

136 FOUR BUILDING SYSTEMS. Particular uses of each building system have to be established before these relationships can be plotted: e.g. the particular use of concrete may in fact be more complex and feminine than the use of steel. Then the functional aspects have to be mapped in the same semantic space, and the two mappings compared.

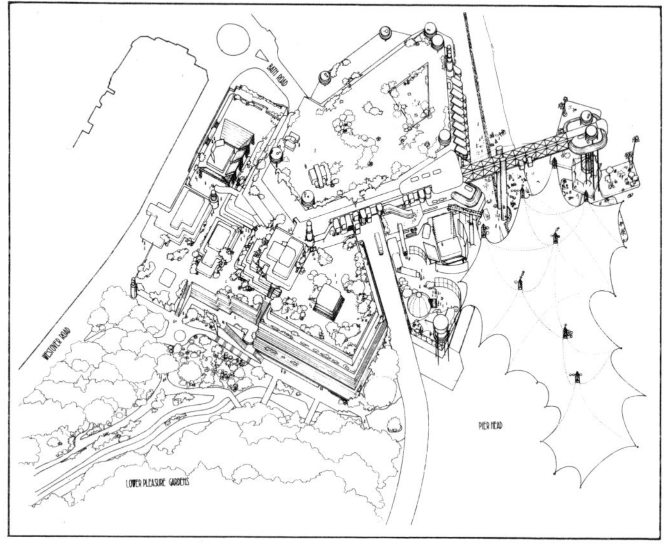

137 ARCHIGRAM, *Bournemouth Scheme,* 1971, uses four different building systems semantically: the tent-like forms signify ephemeral beach activity, the wandering stepped forms signify large-scale collective activity (department store), the fragmented individual objects are the conventional sign for amusement park, and the linear spine classifies circulation. These sytems are then modified or distorted to articulate further meaning: the linear spine indents to accept plastic pod-like rooms and changes into a lattice girder as it goes out over the water.

SCHIZO

The split functions of mixed development have rarely, if ever, been expressed in so split-minded a way as in the *casa per uffici e abitazioni* recently completed in the Via Romagna at Rome, 1, designed by the three brothers Passarelli: three floors of parking out of sight below ground, an open ground floor concourse, three office floors of the sleekest curtain walling in black steel following the street lines, and finally four floors of crazily expressed hanging gardens punched askew. Rudolph stands on Mies. The quadruple columns (ducts running centrally between them) stand proud as pilotis, are enveloped in curtaining and are threaded through balconies. The obvious merit of this mixture aesthetically is that it develops the accrued confusion of history: Roman wall, neo-Romanesque church, 2, shuttered palazzos. Like so many Italian schemes, it all seems balanced, even academic, in section, 3. How was it designed? Perhaps the brothers split it: Vincenzo the flats, Luca the offices and Fausto the car park—a new Adelphi.

TEA

138 PASSARELLI BROTHERS, *Multi-use structure,* Rome, 1965. The concrete and hanging vines classify the flats, the black steel curtain wall indicates office, and below ground, exposed concrete articulates parking. Termed 'Schizo' in this item by *Architectural Review,* and attacked by modernists for its impurity, the building nonetheless makes basic distinctions which are obscured in Purist design.

buildings), so its use hardly ensures that same sincerity which preoccupied the pioneers of the style. Furthermore the 'Masters of Modern Architecture' (I take the phrase from a series of books) have become like the consumer products Coca-Cola, Xerox, and Ford, each with their own house style and corporate brand image. They did not intend this of course, but since they couldn't advertise and since they had to work within a consumer society, the main way of selling their reputation was to develop a single recognisable style which could be purveyed through magazines, books and TV. In short, their authenticity, and their sincerity itself, became a marketable commodity, just as that of Picasso and Ché Guevara did in other fields.

The followers of the 'masters' are led in the same direction, with the result that we can now recognise the Safdie style, the brand marks of Kurokawa and Tange, the Stirling manner, and so forth. How does a client or committee know which one to pick? They choose from books or articles which show his style distinguished from those of competitors. Originality and distinctiveness are saleable items.

The result of this hidden process, of the marketing of reputations, has been to produce a recognisable style of the elite, middle-class architects: it tends towards univalence because of the pressures toward consistency. It is made up from repetitive geometrics, divorced from most metaphors except that of the machine, and purged
139 of vulgarity and the signs common to semiotic groups

139 PAOLO SOLERI, *Arcosanti,* Cordes Junction, Arizona, 1972–7. Restaurant block and accommodation to left and bell foundry and great arch to the right, with housing on either side (semi-circular windows). The Roman-like pattern making, squares, circles and flat masonry walls, is not tied to any semantic system, either historical or internal to the scheme. The formal play is pleasurable, but it doesn't relate to anything other than the grand ecological dreams of Soleri.

other than that of architects. The environment which is created by such a situation is one where every building is a monument to the architect's consistency, rather than appropriate to the job or the urban setting.

The issues involved are obviously complex. An architect must, to a certain extent, develop his own way of doing things, his own details and mannerisms; but these no longer guarantee or signify authenticity as they tended to do before the avant-garde was incorporated into consumer society. And if this practice now produces essentially boring, idiosyncratic sculpture, oversimplified in a single language, then today the architect's sincerity can be measured by his ability to design in a plurality of styles. Consistency equals unconscious hypocrisy, (or, occasionally, conscious elitism).

140 KIYONORI KIKUTAKE, *Tokoen Hotel,* Kaike Spa, Yonago, 1963–4. Boardrooms and conference rooms in the first floor, an open deck, two levels of hotel rooms, stairway and restaurant – all receive distinctive formal treatment which is only slightly less Japanese than the garden. (Kiyonori Kikutake).

PART THREE
Post-Modern Architecture

Recent departures

Several architects are moving beyond modern architecture in a tentative way, either adapting a mixture of modernist styles, or mixing these with previous modes. The results as yet are not convincing enough to speak of a totally new approach and style; they are evolutionary, not a radical departure. And it is in the nature of the case that practising architects now in their forties and trained in modernism can only make hesitant, evolutionary changes. When the present students of architecture start practising, we should begin to see much more convincing examples of radical eclecticism, because it is only this group which is really free enough to try their hand at any possible style – ancient, modern, or hybrid.

A few Japanese architects, Kurokawa, Kikutake and Isozaki among them, have on occasion produced work in several different styles, and single buildings which use various aesthetic systems in a semantic way. Also they have been able to incorporate a traditional language without necessarily being coy or ironic. Why they, unlike Westerners, have been able to be modern *and* traditional without compromising either language remains something of a mystery. Partly it is explained by the persistence of traditional Japanese culture in all areas, and the absence of a revolutionary avant-garde which establishes its credentials by inverting those of the previous generation. But also it is due to the Japanese sophistication towards signs: they have traditionally absorbed alien cultures, or modified the Chinese to their own purposes. Whatever the explanation, the results are there as a lesson to pluralist societies. The architect can design tea-ceremony rooms in a straightforward, sensitive way, or push the latest technology to its expressive limits.

140 Kikutake, in his Tokoen Hotel, has used a version of the Torii gate to acknowledge the entrance, and has employed traditional bracket construction – but in concrete not wood – to articulate the main public areas. The hotel rooms near the top mix tatami proportions and modern architecture; while the restaurant on the roof is under a gentle curve, in blue tile, that manages to recall traditional roof forms and modern hyperbolic parabolas (which in fact it is). Two different structural systems and two aesthetics thus give a legibility and dynamism missing in Western modern architecture.

Kurokawa's Odakyu Drive-In Restaurant is similar in its use of mixed systems. Again the traditional bracket construction is a departure point for the joint, but here the joint has exploded to such prominence that it has
141 swallowed the building and, conversely, the building has
142 swallowed the joint. This witty piece of advertising architecture is in the best roadside tradition – a gigantic metaphor proclaiming its function. The red tent, slung

141 KISHO KUROKAWA

141, 142 KISHO KUROKAWA, *Odakyu Drive-in Restaurant*, Otome, 1969. A giant, white space frame is punctuated by little white and red explosions – tube joints that are reminiscent of the traditional Japanese bracket construction. As Kurokawa said 'the joint swallows the building and the building swallows the joint'. The centre one is actually encased in glass like a religious relic. The red tent and brown, rusted steel, again reminiscent of traditional forms, articulate two different functions. The overall striking image is a conventional sign for roadside stands – *see also* 67, 78. (Kisho Kurokawa Associates).

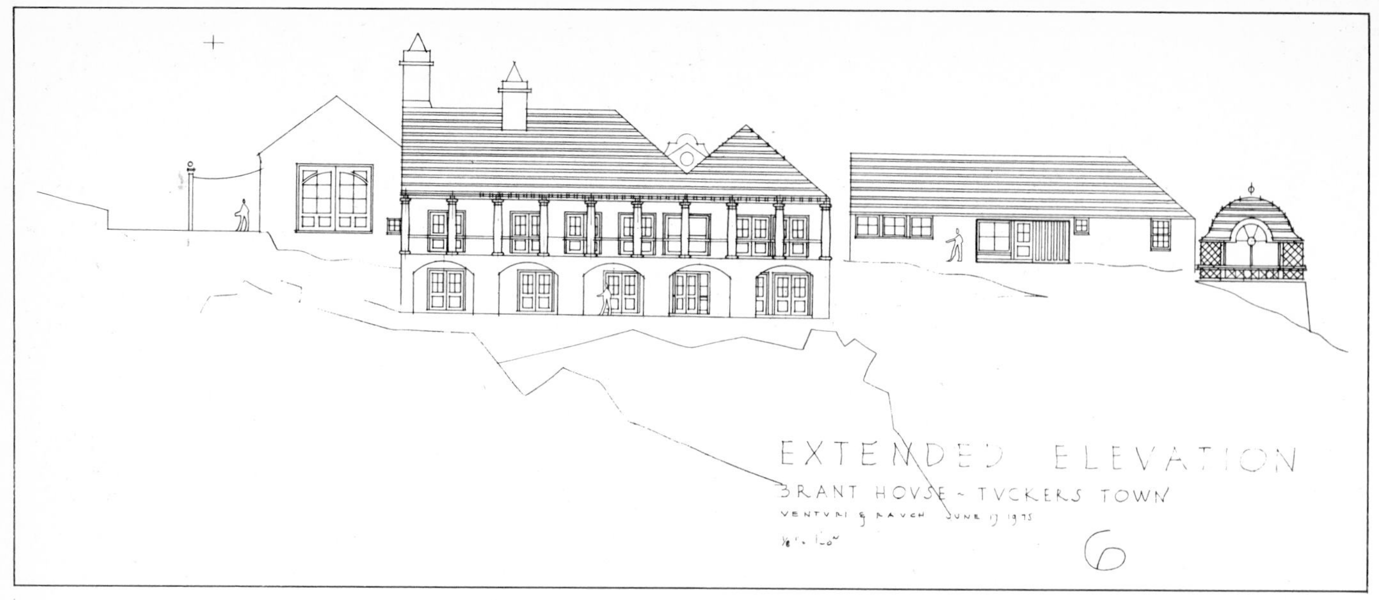

143 VENTURI and RAUCH, *Brandt House,* Tuckertown, Bermuda, 1975. The absorption of different codes into 'the difficult whole'. The tendency of eclecticism is to degenerate into negative pastiche and for the recognisable parts to dominate over and fragment the whole. Here the Belvedere, House and Garden Style and Modernism set up a jangle which is welcome in a leisure retreat – and that very rare genre, positive, self-conscious pastiche. Note the way a cupola sinks, a chimney falls off and windows syncopate against columns, all very . . .

144–147 ROBERT STERN and JOHN HAGMANN, *Residence for an Academical Couple,* Washington, Connecticut, 1974. Scaled-down Palladian makes overtures to the kind of building which gets revived in America every so often. White trim mouldings frame windows and act as symbolic pediment. The one over the door is, like Lucille Ball's, a raised eyebrow, but here it is even more surprised. The strong yellow surfaces recall the painted houses of Scandinavia and Russia, and contrast with the surrounding landscape, rich green in summer, white in winter. Space is layered tightly around the entrance and flows out into the landscape on the other side. The historical references are as academical as the couple who live there. (Edmund H. Stoecklein).

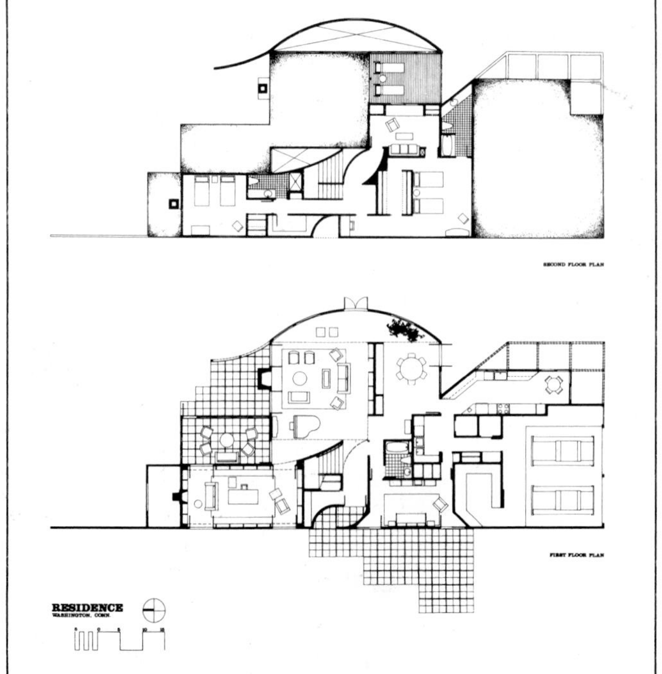

148 CHARLES MOORE and WILLIAM TURNBULL, *Faculty Club,* Santa Barbara, 1968. A medley of diverse signs tightly controlled by geometry. Punched-out walls, which are lit from behind suggest a rich layering of space and a certain mystery as to its extent. Neon banners, tapestry and a chandelier both support and mock the atmosphere of a gentlemen's club.

149 CAMPBELL, ZOGOLOVITCH, WILKINSON and GOUGH, *Phillips West 2, Residences and Offices,* London, 1976. This team of young architects is heading towards radical eclecticism without having yet arrived; here mixed genres and materials articulate the various functions of auction rooms, house and offices.

under the top joints, signifies outdoor activities, in this case a beer garden, while the plug-in capsule of brown steel signifies the main dining room.

Minoru Takeyama, another young Japanese architect, has pushed the use of popular, commercial codes even further in what is perhaps the most convincing Pop building yet designed from within the architectural
83 tradition. His Ni-ban-Kahn makes use of gigantic super-
graphics, optical patterns, written signs, and combines these commercial codes with a geometric discipline and volumetric expression more common in the high game of serious architecture. Architect's architecture and commercial motifs can be combined without compromising either code: in fact their mutual confrontation is a positive gain for both sides. The resultant hybrid, like all inclusive architecture, is not easily subverted by an ironic attack, an unsympathetic viewpoint, because it balances and reconciles opposed meanings. Instead of gaining a tenuous integration by denial, by excluding inharmonious meanings in a search for consistency, this inclusive architecture absorbs conflicting codes in an attempt to create 'the difficult whole'.

This phrase, borrowed from Robert Venturi, should not
144- be regarded as a facile panacea, as his own work shows.
147 It is considerably more difficult to design works which
unify disparate material than to unify already homogeneous meanings and styles; just as it is more difficult to write a tragedy than a farce. By the same token, an inclusive architecture brings much more of our personality and behaviour into focus; just as tragedy articulates a greater wealth of experience than any other genre.[15] The rare, inclusive building – as rare as the true tragedy (most are melodramas) – does not sublimate unattractive aspects of the world. It can include ugliness, decay, banality, austerity, without becoming depressing. It can confront harsh realities of climate, or politics without suppression. It can articulate a bleak metaphysical view of man – Greek architecture and that of Le Corbusier – without either evasion or bleakness.[16] The extraordinary power of tragedy when it is really tragic, or inclusive architecture when it really unifies disparate material, is its disinterested fulfilment. The particular motivation or 'interests' of men are momentarily dropped as they watch a configuration of particularly disturbing events unfold – murders, betrayals, slow disintegration – they watch these monstrosities with detached pleasure, as long as they are balanced or reconciled within an overall tragic pattern. The catharsis this can produce, irrespective of whether it is looked at psychologically (I. A. Richards), or metaphysically (Nietzsche), is of a higher order than the reactions produced by other genres. Inclusive architecture and tragedy, simply, are the pinnacles of expressive modes: there is nothing else as rich, mature and honest towards the complexities of life.

Having staked out grandiose claims for such work, it is unfortunate not to be able to illustrate it with convincing modern examples. But, again, only the
first steps have been taken in this direction, and one doesn't 149
expect them to be accomplished or perfect. Certain buildings of Le Corbusier definitely articulate this kind of experience, but they do so with a Purist language purged of symbolic signs, writing and vulgarity. By contrast, the buildings of Venturi and his team use an inclusive language without attempting much of a reconciliation between opposed meanings. Only one architect manages to be convincingly profound with a hybrid language, Gaudí;

150 RALPH ERSKINE, *Byker Wall,* Newcastle, 1974. Designed while in consultation with the community, this scheme uses a mixture of materials to break down the scale of a potentially massive wall. Brick is used in lower floors, corrugated metal and asbestos in upper ones. Wooden balconies with various shields create semi-private spaces and divide up the whole facade in an unregimented manner. (Bill Toomey/Architectural Press).

151, 152 HERB GREENE, *Prairie House,* Norman, Oklahoma, 1962. Shingle, wood slates and corrugated metal undulate over this house – an *ad hoc* mixture of readily available materials. Called variously The Armadillo, or Preying Mantis, Greene insists that it looks like a mother hen protecting her young (and also a 'wounded creature'). He is one of the few architects to consciously take responsibility for the metaphors in his building (which doesn't mean we have to accept them). (Tim Street-Porter).

but before discussing him, I'd like to instance several examples of this language itself since it is the precondition for an inclusive architecture.

In general terms it can be described as radical eclecticism, or adhocism.[17] Various parts, styles or sub-systems (existing in a previous context) are used in a new, creative synthesis. Radical eclecticism stresses the aspect that these parts must find a semantic justification; eclecticism in itself is a senseless shuffling of styles, as incoherent as Purism, its opposite. Adhocism stresses the aspect that these parts must be unified creatively for a specific purpose (the definition of *ad hoc*). Several recent architec-
150-152, 156, 157 tural examples make it clear what this language looks like. It is variegated rather than homogeneous, witty rather than sombre, messy rather than clean, picturesque but not necessarily without a classical, geometric order (usually it is made from several orders in contrast).

153 WIMMENAUER, SZABO, KASPAR and MEYER, *City superstructure above Dusseldorf,* model, 1969. A spatial city to be built over the old one without destroying it. The glass tube contrasts emphatically with the eighteenth-century building, too emphatically for most people. But if continual destruction of old buildings is to be avoided, then such *ad hoc* juxtapositions will have to be made in certain areas. The oppositions often make two rather mediocre buildings more interesting.

154 HOUSE on 309 STEINER STREET, San Francisco, c. 1890. What is often called the 'Queen Anne Style' was the last great attempt to merge different styles, and incorporate disparate material. In America this hybrid style was much more developed than in England, where it originated, because of the pragmatism and pluralism of the States. The wooden houses of San Francisco, Los Angeles, Texan cities, Savannah and Atlanta go far beyond the tentative eclecticism of today. Visually they are analogues of a Braque collage: balustrade rhythms are broken up and repeated in different places; pediments are slammed through each other; the texture of clapboard is set off against decorative plasterwork; open bay windows are placed in contrast with closed, flat planes; large curves are set against straight lines. Queen Anne was the most dynamic formal system apart from Art Nouveau, and was only weak on a semantic level. (Thomas Aidala and Curt Bruce, *The Great Houses of San Francisco,* Alfred A. Knopf, Inc.)

155, 156 BRUCE GOFF, *Bavinger House,* Norman, Oklahoma, 1957. A continuous spiral of space is surrounded by sandstone and rubble picked up on the site. A mast and steel cables lifted from boat technology and nearby oilfields hold up the roof. The use of materials *ad hoc* creates an interesting contrast between the organic and prefabricated. On the interior, living areas are placed in 'bowls' which are then covered with carpet and fish net. The ultimate *ad hoc* improvisation is the light fixture – a bomber blister taken off a World War Two aircraft. (Bruce Goff).

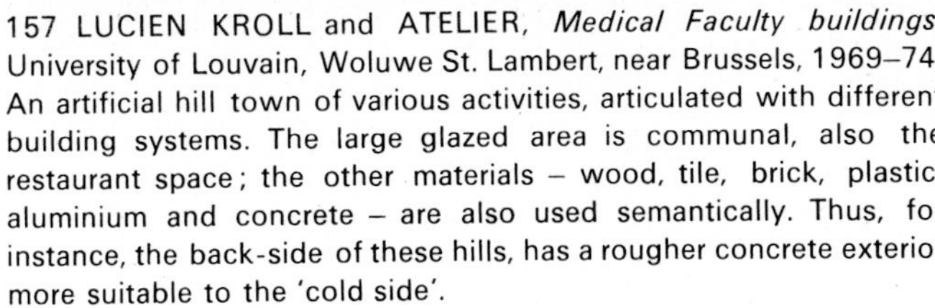

157 LUCIEN KROLL and ATELIER, *Medical Faculty buildings,* University of Louvain, Woluwe St. Lambert, near Brussels, 1969–74. An artificial hill town of various activities, articulated with different building systems. The large glazed area is communal, also the restaurant space; the other materials – wood, tile, brick, plastic, aluminium and concrete – are also used semantically. Thus, for instance, the back-side of these hills, has a rougher concrete exterior more suitable to the 'cold side'.

158 LUCIEN KROLL and ATELIER, *View of two residential hills.* The *ad hoc* use of familiar elements – greenhouses, pitched roof, chimneys – signifies the more private areas. The variety and detail simulate the piecemeal decisions and additions to buildings made over time. Most new buildings do not incorporate this ageing process.

A key *ad hoc* building group, perhaps the largest built to date, is the students' residence and social zone at Louvain University, just outside Brussels. Designed with the aid of Lucien Kroll (who acted as orchestra leader for the various design groups), this set of structures resembles
84, a child's building-block hill town more than a traditional
57- group of university buildings. The reason is simply that
59 many students participated in its design, and they used small bits of plastic foam in working out a model. They shuffled these bits around, combining various functions, such as individual rooms with restaurant. But disputes arose and the inevitable specialisation of teams led to an impossible fragmentation. Kroll reorganised these teams several times, letting them become more familiar with each other's problems, until a possible solution was in sight. Not until then did he draw up the plans and sections which made it workable.

The resultant buildings show a complexity and richness of meaning that usually takes years to achieve and is the
158 result of many inhabitants making small adjustments over time. The fact that a simulation of such piecemeal tinkering and pluralism can be built in from the beginning through such a process, should not be underrated. It takes, of course, the commitment and understanding that Kroll and his group had from the start; but the process is definitely generalisable, and similar results have been achieved elsewhere with similar processes of consultation, if not participation – Ralph Erskine and his team at Byker, for instance.

Kroll's orchestration even went so far as allowing the builders a certain improvisation while constructing. They
changed the siding of one building from rough rubble 159
stonework to brick and tile as the work progressed, so this building seems to grow up from the ground like a variegated tree. The students wished to combine functions while distinguishing them visually, so five different building systems were used – tile, plastic, aluminium and glass, wood, and concrete – in a finely-grained patchwork. No explicit semantic modelling was used, as far as I know, but the parts bespeak their use with a certain eloquence and mutual toleration. Perhaps this was due to Kroll himself, as participation won't automatically produce such sensitivity. There was clearly an aesthetic intention consciously brought to bear on the scheme at some point; and it is this skill, which has been delicately keyed into the process without dominating it, that distinguishes this result of participation from others, and from the very large self-build movement.

159 VIEW ACROSS MAIN PIAZZA showing builders' contribution to design. The rocks grow up from the ground and change into brick and then tile, a transformation reminiscent of Gaudí's work.

Perhaps participation has been oversymbolised. Kroll boasts that no two bedroom windows next to each other are the same; and when I was there in 1976 I found parts of the building had graffiti and political slogans written on them before they were being used. It was as if the street art of May '68 was being preapplied down at the factory. Perhaps the scheme may be overarticulated and somewhat too fussy in its insistent attempt to humanise and individualise.

Nonetheless, the spirit of the place really captures the feeling of what *ad hoc* design can be – a continually renewed improvisation on themes coming from every possible source. There are pitched roofs here which tumble about the roof-scape of an amoeboid community building; other popular signs, such as trellis-work, greenhouse sheds, and primitive figurative sculpture, punctuate the main blob of the scheme (one has to apply new architectural terms to these units – perhaps 'hills' is a better word). The syncopation of various materials over the surface of these blob-hills can only be described as rich and riotous; tumultuous in the detail and violent in the whole – and yet still very personal and small-scaled. It is a kind of language very appropriate to student life and desires (at least *some* desires). I'm sure certain critics are going to condemn this as the totalitarianism of enforced participation, where there is no normalised architecture for the student who just wants to be his ordinary, privatised self. Indeed, perhaps improvisation has gone too far, spread all over the site in every detail. But this excess is the price often paid for innovating a new process of design, and there is nothing inherent in the process which precludes ordinary building for those who really want it. They will just have to make their voices heard in the future as the university continues to expand.

Multivalent architecture

The direction that Kroll and these other architects are moving towards is a pluralistic language which incorporates traditional and modern elements, vernacular and high art meanings. The Japanese designers, Charles Moore, the Venturi team, Bruce Goff, and countless individuals building their own handmade houses, do not yet constitute a single coherent tradition; but they have enough in common to make a very loosely defined group departing from the orthodoxies of the modern movement. They find support, if not identity of approach, in the
emergent philosophies of the ecological movement, 160
'small is beautiful', intermediate technology, and the

160 STEVE BAER, *Solar heated Zome structure,* Corrales, New Mexico, 1974. The ecological movement is producing systems which sometimes have semantic implications. Although these haven't yet been absorbed into the normal house, they may become as ubiquitous as the chimney or roof. Here walls lower to the ground, when desirable, to reveal water-filled barrels which soak up the sun on a bright day, and keep the house warm for two or three sunless days. (Zomeworks Corporation).

general trend towards decentralisation which is being called for around the world. These last movements are neutral concerning a new language of architecture, they aren't concerned with the way buildings communicate one way or another, but their underlying pluralism is to be welcomed.

If this pluralism is going to amount to anything it will really have to become more tough-minded. The architect will have be trained in four or five different styles and trained as an anthropologist, or at least a good journalist, to learn and be able to use the particular architectural codes that prevail among the subcultures that persist in any large city. He will have to learn the particular metaphors and symbolic signs which have a short-lived potency, and the slow-changing traditional signs, and use all these with wit and precision. This is not going to be an easy thing to do because the other part of his training, in the new technologies and abstract methodologies of planning, will inevitably remove him, as they have done in the past, from the users of his buildings. He will continue to have a professional ideology induced by the modern movement on a world-wide scale; he will respond to formal inventions coming from Italy and Japan, theory that emanates from London and New York, and individual practice coming from everywhere. He will build for multinational and large corporations and indefinable clients; he will still love the manipulation of pure form and the high game of Architects' Architecture. All these forces will alienate him from the people who ultimately use his buildings and there is little hope of changing these forces (barring the collapse of international communications and all economies, not a very happy solution).

A realistic assessment of the situation suggests that schizophrenia is the only intelligent approach. The architect should be trained as a radical schizophrenic (everything must be radical today), always looking two ways with equal clarity: towards the traditional slow-changing codes and particular ethnic meanings of a neighbourhood, and towards the fast-changing codes of architectural fashion and professionalism. If he doesn't make this schizophrenia quite explicit and incorporate it as part of his basic training, then he will be an inadvertent victim of one pressure or the other.

On the other hand, if he does adopt this dual approach, his enjoyment of architecture might actually increase, as he becomes more responsible for its various meanings. The more he can know about how people will react to the forms he uses, the more he can confidently use and decode them. The pleasure of manipulating various languages will easily repay the effort at learning them.

Ultimately however, it is the way a language is used that matters, the actual messages sent as much as the particular language used. Obviously if an architect has nothing important to say, his facility with communication is just going to advertise this fact clearly; so ideology, and ideas, are also preconditions for effective discourse. A multivalent architecture, opposed to a univalent building, combines meanings imaginatively so that they fuse and *modify* each other. A multivalent architecture, like the inclusive building, makes use of the *full arsenal of communicational means,* leaving out no area of experience, and suppressing no particular code (although of course any building is inevitably limited in range).

The only architect I could say really uses a pluralist language to produce multivalent works, Antonio Gaudí, has sometimes been classified as an Art Nouveau designer.

161 ANTONIO GAUDI, *Bell towers of Sagrada Familia cathedral,* Barcelona, 1884–1926. The tops of these towers are often seen as Cubism before its time, because of the smashed up, geometric tiles and collaged patterns. But they are representational as well, with written signs – 'Hosanna, Excelsis' – and floral imagery. The tapered, parabolic form was also advanced for its time.

The problem with this classification is that it obscures Gaudí's universality, not to say peculiarity. He was a man deeply committed to Barcelona's separatist movement, and to 'modernismo', its artistic expression, as well as more general social issues, such as workers' control and Christian humanism.

Gaudí's version of Art Nouveau was highly inclusive, even cannibalistic: it swallowed Moorish elements, tiles and domical vaults; it absorbed Gothic motifs, buttresses, pinnacles, and stained glass; it borrowed nature's plants
87 and animals, metaphors of any living creature; and incorporated emergent forms of engineering (the parabola and hyperbolic parabola were practically invented by Gaudí). Spatially it flowed and curved around solid elements, while structurally it not only articulated the lines for force, but dramatised them as twisting muscles and tendons. Symbolically, his work followed the local Christian and social meanings existing in Barcelona at the time. And Gaudí was not even intimidated by vulgarity – he'd write various slogans across the tops of his building, early Cubist advertisements. There wasn't a communicational mode Gaudí didn't use at least once.

163 His Casa Batllo, finished in 1907, is a particularly multivalent work, where meanings modify one another. You come upon it near the corner of a main boulevard in Barcelona, past a phalanx of plane trees on the Paseo de
Gracia. On one side is a typical nineteenth-century apart- 162
ment block in the classical style; on the other, the stepped shops and polychromy of another Art Nouveau building. Gaudí has filled this hole with a building that respects the street facade and unites the two adjoining structures, (or at least did until one of them was added to). He also adopts a variation of the window treatments on either side.

On inspecting the entrace facade, you can discover a series of metaphors and symbolic signs. The balconies stare back like so many death masks or skulls. The middle part of the architecture also recalls vegetable and marine metaphors, with some people seeing it as a violent blue sea breaking over rocks, which then turn into kelp (the codes of Barcelona are, after all, sensitive to the sea).

The lower two floors adopt a related organic metaphor of skeletons and bones, (the architecture was known as 'the house of bones'), and you can see this exoskeleton go internal on two sides of the third floor. A recent designer has incorporated a wandering, blue neon sign suggesting, if we continue the metaphor, that the 'legs have varicose veins' – a rather ludicrous example of the way multivalent architecture forces meanings to modify each other.

It is quite possible to see these 'bones' as tendons, or a ductile metaphor of wax or lava. If a mixed metaphor is

162 ANTONIO GAUDI, *Casa Batllo,* Barcelona, 1904–6. The building picks up the street facade on either side and makes variations on similar window themes. The Art Nouveau movement in Barcelona, called *Modernismo,* had a strong, popular base in this city and two other examples of it can be seen in this block – one to the extreme left, the other next to the Casa Batllo.

more dramatic than a single, obvious one, then it is Gaudi's particular strength to find a multiplicity of meanings for these mixtures.

For instance, they divide the architecture into three main functional parts (following the classical convention): a base of two floors with the bone/wax metaphor which can denote 'shops', 'entrance' and 'main apartment'; a shaft of four floors in the marine/mask metaphor which can denote 'similar apartments of a lesser nature'; finally a capital, a roof in the dragon metaphor which can denote 'roof garden, water tanks, skylight, mechanical equipment'. Thus strange, regional codes are used to signify different functions and break up a large apartment block into identifiable and personal areas. How far this is from the recent practice of anonymous slab blocks it is not necessary to emphasise.

The pre-eminent role of the architect is to articulate our environment, not only so we can comprehend it literally, but also so we can find it psychologically nourishing, create meanings we hadn't even imagined were possible.

In this sense the overall message, or symbol, of the Casa Batllo is truly extraordinary: it articulates meanings which are much more profound than the surface metaphors of which it is composed. For a long time I puzzled over the meaning of the roof dragon – that sleeping monster sprawled out at the top who looks down on the passerby with one eye lazily half open. The ceramic tile of 164
what appears at first its tail (the three-dimensional cross) shades slowly from golden orange on the left to blue green on the right. Gaudí was a very devout Christian and he announced the fact with the cross and initials of the Holy Family encrusted on the cylinder. But what sort of Christianity is this? I had assumed the dragon was a typical Art Nouveau conceit, taken perhaps from Chinese garden walls which undulate this way, but I couldn't see its relation to a religious message. Was it a kind of Tao-Christianity, a form of nature-worship akin to pantheism? I assumed this until I was told the conventional reference to these signs. The missing clue was supplied by the architect David Mackay, and the correct interpretation came into focus with all the vividness of a suddenly solved crime.

St George, it turns out, is the patron saint of this city, and Barcelona has always been the centre of a separatist, Catalonian movement. It has its special Catalan dialect and has always sparked off regional groups and extreme individualists. Anarchism has had a foothold there: Picasso, Sert, Salvador Dali, Miro, are some of the more pronounced individualists. When you walk along the back

163 ANTONIO GAUDI, *Casa Batllo,* facade. Bones and lava at the base, death masks and undulating sea in the middle, and dragon looking down sleepily at the top. These metaphors articulate the different interior functions. (Escuela Tecnica Superior de Arquitectura de Barcelona).

streets and main commercial avenues and eat the highly sophisticated sea food, you realise that this city is European, not just Spanish; it has had Mediterranean roots (and routes) for several thousand years. The nationalist movement to which Gaudí belonged was trying to assert its independence from Spanish domination. The Casa Batllo then apparently represents this struggle in its metaphors: the dragon – Spain – is being slain by that three-dimensional cross wielded by Barcelona's patron saint. The bones and skulls refer to the dead martyrs who have been victimised in the struggle.[18] All this in an apartment building! But coded with enough subtlety to be apparent only to those who care to read it in depth. The deeper symbol, the knowledge of which transforms your whole view of the building, is not absolutely necessary in order to grasp its more obvious meanings. But like multivalent works in other fields it speaks to many different people on different levels.

These kinds of work, the six major tragedies of Shakespeare for instance, have the power to engage the mind and open our imaginations to new meaning. They are catalytic, provocative and creative, stimulating each generation to reach beyond its familiar abstractions and discover new interpretations; whereas the univalent work is reductive, dull, and ultimately repressive. A multivalent architecture remains alive because its meanings are so related as to allow new paths to be discovered between them. Finally, then, it is because of its effect on us that such architecture is mandatory – because it will shape us in multiple ways and speak to various groups, to the whole spectrum of society rather than just one of its elites. In the long run we are transformed by what we experience and inhabit; and the quality of architecture affects the quality of our minds at least as much as any other artefact we make.

No doubt many architects are now as disenchanted with modernism as the public, and a new paradigm, or theory, is beginning to form. This paradigm is still loosely defined and it doesn't yet enjoy a large consensus, but the outlines of what it is becoming are clear, particularly to the generation of architects now in their thirties. The next five years promise to be extremely interesting for architects, as the paradigm takes shape – but also probably confused and uncertain. The adage 'may you be cursed to live in interesting times' is good warning for the architect now about to practise, because he will invariably spend a large part of his time fighting battles of taste, with differing publics. But this is not necessarily a bad thing. After all, the modern movement itself came into existence through struggle, and it won't exit without a fight. Every change in paradigm entails struggle, and the paradox facing our generation of architects is that it has to go backwards to previous theories, and reweave several strands which have been cut away, in order to go forward.

We must go back to a point where architects took responsibility for rhetoric, for how their buildings communicated intentionally, how 'decorum' and *bienséance* were consciously achieved, and then combine insights from such a study with a relevant theory of semiotics, so that an updated rhetoric can be consciously taught along with other specialities – no, as the unifying agent of these other disciplines. For an architect's primary and final role is to express the meanings a culture finds significant, as well as elucidate certain ideas and feelings that haven't previously reached expression. The jobs that too often take up his energy might be better done by engineers and sociologists, but no other profession is specifically responsible for articulating meaning and seeing that the environment is sensual, humorous, surprising and coded as a readable text. This is the architect's job and pleasure, not, let us hope, ever again his 'problem'.

164 THE DRAGON, often incorporated in Gaudí's work, finally meets his fate.

NOTES

1 See Mies van der Rohe, 'Industrialized Building', originally printed in the magazine, *G*, Berlin, 1924, and reprinted in Ulrich Conrads, *Programmes and Manifestoes on 20th-Century Architecture*, London, 1970, p. 81.

2 See Manfredo Tafuri, 'L'Architecture dans le boudoir', *Oppositions 3*, New York, 1974, p. 45 and note p. 60. Tafuri claims that the 'accusations of fascism hurled at Rossi mean little, since his attempts at the recovery of an ahistoricizing form exclude verbalizations of its content and any compromise with the real'. This escape clause is of course impossible; all form will be looked at historically and have conventional associations tied to it, and Rossi's work cannot escape this 'compromise with the real' any more than all other architecture.

3 Peter and Alison Smithson, *Architectural Design*, October 1969, p. 560.

4 Peter Smithson, *Architectural Design*, May 1975, p. 272.

5 Alison and Peter Smithson, *L'Architecture d'aujourd'hui*, January 1975, p. 9.

6 See Tom Wolfe, *The New Journalism*, Picador, London, 1975, pp. 54–6, and my article 'The Rise of Post-Modern Architecture', *Architectural Association Quarterly*, London, Summer 1976, pp. 7–14.

7 For the call to morality see Sigfried Giedion, *Space, Time and Architecture*, Cambridge, Mass., 1971, pp. 214, 291–308. For the 'Heroic Period', see Peter and Alison Smithson, issue of *Architectural Design*, December 1965.

8 Sant' Elia's 'Manifesto', July 11, 1914, is quoted from *Futurismo 1909–1919*, exhibition of Italian Futurism, organised by Northern Arts and the Scottish Arts Council, 1972, catalogue, p. 49.

9 A more rigorous comparison of architecture to language is made by architectural semioticians, who substitute technical terms for these imprecise analogues. For our general purpose however, the analogies will suffice, as long as we don't take them too literally.

10 A point made by Umberto Eco in 'Function and Sign: Semiotics and Architecture', published in *Structures Implicit and Explicit*, Graduate School of Fine Arts University of Pennsylvania, Vol. 2, 1973. Republished in our anthology edited by Geoffrey Broadbent, Dick Bunt and myself, *Signs, Symbols and Architecture*, Wiley, to appear in 1978.

11 See Umberto Eco, 'A Componential Analysis of the Architectural Sign/Column', in *Semiotica 5*, Number 2, 1972, Mouton, The Hague, pp. 97–117.

12 See for instance Herbert Gans' description of the five major 'taste cultures' in his *Popular Culture and High Culture*, Basic Books, New York, 1974, pp. 69–103.

13 See G. L. Hersey, 'J. C. Loudon and Architectural Associationism', *Architectural Review*, August, 1968, pp. 89–92.

14 The use of 'naturally' begs the important semiotic issue of exactly *how* natural a sign can be. They all depend on coding, and therefore convention. But the issue is too complex to be treated here. See Umberto Eco, *A Theory of Semiotics*, Indiana University Press, Bloomington, 1976, pp. 191–221.

15 The organising powers of tragedy and its pre-eminence is discussed by I. A. Richards in his *Principles of Literary Criticism*, 1925. See the Harvest Book edition, Harcourt, Brace and World, New York, no date, pp. 245–50.

16 I have partly explored this notion in *Le Corbusier and the Tragic View of Architecture*, London and Cambridge, Mass., 1973, but my discussion of tragedy there was severely curtailed.

17 In *Adhocism*, New York and London, 1972, Nathan Silver and I showed many examples of various styles and building systems being lifted from their former contexts and being put together *ad hoc* in a new synthesis. Arthur Koestler has illuminated the general principle involved in his *Act of Creation*, London, 1964.

18 This is third-hand information, and a guess on my part. Gaudí told the architect Martorell that the roof represented a dragon being slain; Martorell told his son, Josep Maria, who told his partner, David Mackay, who told me. Given the separatist ideals of *Modernismo* it then seems logical to me that the dragon would represent Spain, the bones and skulls becoming veiled symbols of the Catalan martyrs. Surely many Catalans must have seen it this way, since St George and the dragon appear on other separatist buildings, and Catalan Nationalism was very closely associated with *Modernismo* (for a while its style).

Some critics might say that Gaudí's work is too highly wrought to act as a model for the present city – a veritable zoo of animalistic and other meanings – but the basic lessons are there to follow: a full use of the expressive means, all the modes of communication. In one sense, Gaudí had it easy. He was in a rich traditional society, immersed in everyday Catholic faith, and working at a time (during the *Renaixenca* and *Modernismo*) when architects could use metaphors and symbols as a matter of course, without reflection. Animal and vegetable metaphors cover many *Modernismo* buildings – not just mythic beasts such as the dragon, but domestic ones such as cats and dogs. Thus this culture did a lot of work for Gaudí, something which we can't expect today. And yet in the mass culture of the West, there are many of the same values and forces at work, even if they are finely spread out across society, and operative in a commercial and debased form. They are there, and it is theoretically possible that some individual and group can reweave these disparate aspects together and achieve something as deep and intense as *Modernismo*.

INDEX

Adhocism 7, 84, 92, *92, 93, 94,* 95, 96, 102
appropriateness, *see also* suitability 7, 15, 31, 32, 44, 45, 46, *47,* 48, 58, *58,* 75, 77, *78, 79, 80,* 82, 85, 97
Arendt, Hannah 10
Art Nouveau 7, 72, *93,* 97, 98, 99, *99*
Baer, Steve *97*
Banham, Reyner *72*
Behrens, Peter 26, *26*
Bofill, Ricardo *6,* 21, *49*
Bunshaft, Gordon 19, *19,* 20, *20,* 26, *26*
Campbell, Zogolovitch, Wilkinson and Gough *90*
code, *see also* language and meaning
  architectural 7, *9,* 20, 40, 42, 72, 77, *88,* 90, 101
  commercial 90
  conventional 44, 60
  elitist 12, 21, 48
  fast-changing 58, 97
  interpretation of 16, *42,* 44, 48, 60
  learned 42, 44
  local *42,* 43, 58, 99, 101
  multiple 42
  overcoding 48, *48,* 58
  popular 20, 21, 25, 48, *71,* 90
  short-lived 58
  slow-changing 97
  traditional 42
  undercoding 72
  violation of 44, *66*
  visual 40, 42, 48, 60
Cross, Dixon and Jones *31*
decorated shed 45, *45, 70*
duck 42, *42,* 45, 46, 48, *57,* 62, *70*
eclecticism 63, 66, *69,* 75, 77, 84, *88,* 92, *93*
Eisenman, Peter 73, *73*
Ellul, Jacques 10
ersatz *8, 10,* 12, *12,* 28, 37, 65, *79*
Erskine, Ralph *91,* 95
formalism 19, 45
Foster, Norman *80*
Franzen, Ulrich 19
functionalism 15, *26,* 44, *44,* 62, 63, *72*
Gaudí, Antonio *56,* 90, *96,* 97, 98, *98,* 99, *99, 100,* 101, *101,* 102
Goff, Bruce *94,* 96
Gombrich, E.H. *42,* 77
Graves, Michael *54,* 72
Greene, Herb *92*
Gropius, Walter 31, *40,* 62, 63, 84
handmade houses, *see also* self-build 12, *13,* 72, *72,* 84, 96
Hertzberger, Herman 21, *21*
Hodgkinson, Patrick *30*
Hollein, Hans 32, *32, 33*
hybrid architecture 87, 90
Illich, Ivan 10, 13
Illinois Institute of Technology 15, *16,* 17, *17*
International Style 10, *10,* 14, *71,* 72, 77, 84
Isozaki, Arata 21, *22,* 87
Jacobs, Jane 7, 9
Jameson, Conrad 7
Johnson, Philip 19
Kahn, Louis 70, 72
Kikutake, Kiyonori *86,* 87
kitsch *18,* 19, *71, 79*
Kroll, Lucien *55,* 95, *95,* 96
Kurokawa, Kisho *4,* 40, *40,* 85, 87, *87*
language, *see also* code and meaning 7, 43, 48, 58, 60
  architectural 7, *9,* 15, 16, 19, 21, 22, 23, 26, 28, 60, *62,* 63, *63,* 64, *66,* 96, 97, 102
  cliché 14, *31,* 40, 60, 72, 84
  conventional 44, 75
  grammar 15, 39
  hybrid 72, 90
  inclusive 90, 92
  irony *10,* 20, *32,* 37, 70, 87
  local 37
  message *18, 39,* 99
  phrase 39
  popular 70
  rhetoric *30,* 72, 101
  shared 13, 24, 63
  syntax 39, *61, 69,* 72, *72,* 73
  traditional 87
  word 39, 44, *44,* 60, *61,* 62
Lapidus, Morris *8, 10*
Le Corbusier 9, *18,* 31, 37, 48, *48, 62,* 63, 69, *69,* 70, 84, 90, 102
Loos, Adolf *38,* 60, *61*
MacEwen, Malcolm 10, 12
Mackay, David 99, 102
meaning, *see also* code and language *42,* 44, 45, *45,* 48, 97
  architectural 7, *16,* 20, *20, 22,* 44, 60, 63, 75, 84, *84,* 98
  conventional 75, 77
  inadvertent 15, 77
  intended 7, 13, 46
  multivalent *42,* 45, 46, 99, 101
  natural 75, 77, 78
  opposing 42, 75, *79,* 90
  unintended 15, 19, 20, 21
  univalent 20
Meier, Richard 69, *69*

metaphor
 architectural 22, 40, *40,* 43, 44, 46, *47, 57,* 58, *58,* 60, *63, 82,* 87, 97, *100,* 102
 factory 15, 16, *16, 26,* 31, *31*
 hospital 9, *22,* 31
 inadvertent 58
 intended *92, 82*
 machine 23, *31,* 85
 mixed 42, *42, 43,* 44, 45, 98
 organic 43, 44, 45, 98, 102
 response to 60
 suggested 48, 101
Mies van der Rohe *14,* 15, *15,* 16, *16, 17,* 19, 26, 46, 73, 102
modern architecture 7, 10, 12, *22,* 24, 25, 26, 28, *28,* 32, 37, 40, 44, 48, *67,* 85, 87
 crisis in 10, 12, *12,* 14, 15
 death of 9
modern movement, the 7, 10, 15, 21, 26, *30,* 45, 72, 96, 97, 101
Moore, Charles *89,* 96
Moore and Turnbull *89*
multivalence, *see also* meaning 20, 46, 96, 97, 98, 101
Nash, John 77, 78, *78, 79*
Newman, Oscar *9, 23*
Oakshott, Michael 10
Pacific Design Center 58, *58*
participation 95, 96
Passarelli brothers 84, *85*
Pei, I.M. *18,* 19
Pelli, Cesar 58, *58*
Pessac *62,* 63
Pevsner, Nikolaus 48, 77, 78
Piano and Rogers *30, 50*
pluralism 7, 70, 85, *93,* 95, 96, 97
Portman, John *35*
post-modernism 7
Pruitt-Igoe 9, *9,* 63
Purism 9, *9,* 16, *62,* 63, 84, *85,* 90
radical eclecticism 7, 87, *90,* 92
radical schizophrenia 24, 42, 97
rationalism 9, 10, 14, 15, 45, 58, 63, 73]
Ronchamp chapel 48, *48, 57,* 58
Rossi, Aldo 20, *20,* 102
Saarinen, Eero 26, 46, *47*
Sant' Elia 35, 37, 102
Schumacher, E.F. 10
Scott Brown, Denise 70, *70*
Seifert, Richard *10, 11*
self-build, *see also* handmade houses 13, *13,* 95
semantics, *see also* language and meaning 16, 20, *30,* 39, *61,* 73, 75, 77, 78, *79, 80,* 82, 84, *84, 85,* 87, *93, 95, 97*
semiotics 7, *45, 57, 58,* 65, 78, 101, 102
semiotic group, *see also* taste culture 7, 63, 64, 66, 70, 85
signs
 architectural 7, 16, 17, *18,* 40, *40, 42,* 60, *61, 63,* 64, 66, *89*
 conventional 20, 24, 25, 45, 62, *62,* 63, *67,* 70, 84, 85, *87*
 iconic 45, *45,* 46, 62
 indexical 62
 natural 62, *67, 76,* 77, 102
 popular 58, *63,* 70, 96
 slow-changing 97
 status 25, *63,* 64, 66, 69
 symbolic 45, *45,* 60, 62, 63, 72, 90, 97, 98
 systematically misunderstood 63
 traditional *31,* 63, 97
signification 7, 15, 19, 24, *40,* 45, 48, *61,* 62, 63, 73, 75, *75, 76,* 77, *84,* 90, *95*
Skidmore, Owings and Merrill 19, *19, 20,* 26, *26*
Smithson, Alison and Peter 21, 22, 23, *23,* 24, 102
Soleri, Paolo *85*
Stern and Hagmann *88*
Stirling, James 21, 48, 85
suitability, *see also* appropriateness *74,* 75, 82
Sydney Opera House 42, 43, *43,* 44, 45, 46, 47, *51*
symbolism *9,* 15, 16, 20, *20, 21,* 22, *23, 24,* 37, *42,* 44, 45, 64, 70, *70,* 77, *78, 88,* 98, 99, 101, 102
Tafuri, Manfredo 20, 102
Takeyama, Minoru *53,* 90
Tange, Kenzo *28, 31,* 85
taste culture, *see also* semiotic group 7, 13, 63, 70, 102
Three Orders 39, 60, 62, 75, 77, 78, *79*
 Corinthian 39, 77, 78, *78, 79*
 Doric *14,* 39, *61,* 75, 77, 78
 Ionic 39, 77, 78
TWA building 26, 46, *47,* 58
univalence 15, 19, 25, 46, 85, 101
universality 7, 15, *16,* 62, 98
Utzon, Jorn *42,* 43, 45, 46
values 15, 25, 35, 37, 63, 64, 65, 66, 70
Venturi, Robert *13,* 35, 45, *45,* 46, 62, 70, *70, 71, 88,* 90, 96
Venturi and Rauch *71*
Williams-Ellis, Sir Clough 69, *69*
Wimmenauer, Szabo, Kaspar and Meyer *93*
Wright, Frank Lloyd *18,* 19, 26, *26,* 62, 84
Yamasaki, Minoru *9*